Penguin Books Ltd, Harmondsworth, Middlesex, England
Viking Penguin Inc., 40 West 23rd Street, New York, New York 10010, U.S.A.
Penguin Books Australia Ltd, Ringwood, Victoria, Australia
Penguin Books Canada Ltd, 2801 John Street, Markham, Ontario, Canada L3R 1B4
Penguin Books (N.Z.) Ltd, 182–190 Wairau Road, Auckland 10, New Zealand

First published 1985

Edited and designed by Robert Ditchfield Ltd
Illustrated by Emma Tovey

Acknowledgements
The publishers would like to thank the following contributors and
copyright owners of the colour photographs:
Gillian and Kenneth Beckett (41 below); Una and Denis Green (17, 25,
41 above, 44, 45 above, 48, 53 above right and below right); Bryan
Merrett (4); Diana Saville (5, 9, 29, 32, 37 above and below left, and right,
45 below, 49 above and below, 53 above and below left).

Printed and bound in Italy by New Interlitho, Milan

Typesetting by Keyspools Ltd
Colour separation by RCS Graphics Ltd

Rock Gardens and Alpines

John Warwick

PENGUIN BOOKS

Contents

1. The Site

Alpines grow in the Alps, strictly speaking, but in general terms, together with rock plants, come mostly from all the mountainous regions of the world. In the wild they generally grow in light, open, and exposed positions. The exceptions are those included under rock plants that grow in woodlands (shade) or, because of their relatively small size, can be grown in a limited space. Dwarf bulbs from hot, baked areas in summer to ones that prosper in short turf are often able to grow in our gardens. The high alpines from above the tree line of mountain regions are the pride of the scree, rock garden, sink garden, raised bed, meadow or even bog garden of any home. These, interspersed with larger or faster-growing plants of the lower regions, can give a riot of colour not just in the spring, but throughout the summer and into the autumn. All the conditions of the wild can be emulated in the garden by producing them artificially.

Saxifraga oppositifolia in the Swiss Alps.

Choosing a site

The site should be clear of trees and shrubs to allow the widest range of alpines to grow. If leaves fall in the autumn and cover the site, they will have to be removed by hand a few at a time to prevent botrytis, or rotting of the stems of the small plants underneath. The trees and shrubs should also be far enough away from the prevailing wind, normally from the south-west, to prevent the same problem; and they should not cast shade for more than a short period. Shade cast by building and fences is best kept to a minimum. Plants can be grown in the shade, particularly woodland shade, but too much and the range is limited.

Most gardens which have been established for some years are arranged with a rectangle of lawn covering most of the area, and narrow borders containing

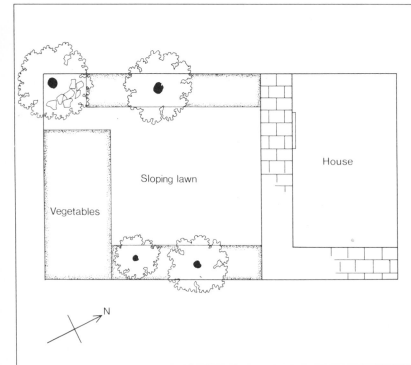

A typical garden showing trees on each side, with two narrow borders beneath them. A large area of grass is bordered at each end by a path round the house, and the vegetable garden at the bottom end. The 'rockery' is often under a tree tucked away from the light as shown in the top left corner of the diagram and frequently made of any hard materials available.

trees, shrubs, herbaceous and bedding plants. A vegetable plot is often at the bottom end, while the house is at the head end.

The site chosen in order to show the options, is a sloping one from the house down to the vegetable garden, with the rear of the house facing almost south. Should your situation be reversed, then use the front garden, or adapt to your particular needs. The site shown is shaded in the early morning, but could catch the late sun if not obstructed by the trees or buildings near the vegetable plot. Very few situations are absolutely ideal, but most offer possibilities. A site that is flat and shaded by fences or walls could catch more light if you build a raised bed, but this cannot, of course, then be a rock garden.

A very small garden is better without a lawn. Pave it and construct raised beds and sink gardens to give maximum variety, with plants growing out of the paving as well. A small garden of say 20 ft (6 m) square should be able to accommodate about four hundred different plants in this way, both horizontally and vertically, especially if they are all relatively small growers.

Alpine and rock plants thrive in a garden.

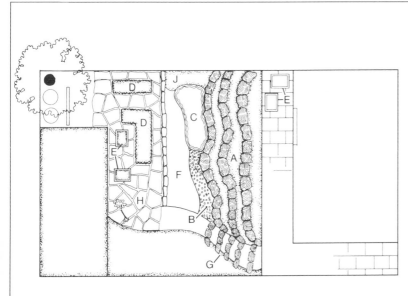

The garden shown opposite transformed into a practical and worthwhile garden. Three trees have been removed, leaving one in the corner. The vegetable plot is left as it was. The border at the top of the diagram is removed, and the one opposite enlarged. A rock garden (A), scree (B), pool (C), raised beds (D), and sink gardens (E), have been added to take up most of the grass area. Area F is the remaining grass which is planted with bulbs with a retaining wall below it. A flight of steps (G) runs down to the paved area with plants growing in it (H) to give a dry walk to the vegetable garden. A bog garden is created by the pond (J) but as a separate unit. The screened off area under the trees has two bins for garden compost.

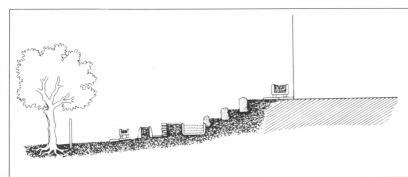

A cross section of the new garden which shows the relative heights of each raised section, and the pool below ground level.

2. Associated Areas

A rock garden is an informal area of the garden, so a formal design or planting must be thought out very carefully before it is placed anywhere near it. Trees and shrubs nearby are also best avoided as they may cast shade and drop their leaves onto the plants; the ornamental trees on the south-east side of the illustration on page 4 have been removed for this reason.

Always bear in mind the other areas of the garden when planning, and draw up rough plans on paper to use as a guide.

Ornamental and fruit trees

Trees to avoid near any construction are flowering cherries, sweet chestnuts and horse chestnuts because of their large and thick leaves. Big forest trees of oak, beech etc. grow too large for a small garden. Birch and elm both have roots close to the soil surface, and no rock garden or other structure must be built near them, as their roots will come up into the structures.

Fruit trees of apples, pears and plums are not suitable. Spraying operations will affect other plants around them, especially the smaller ones. Tar oil wash, for example, will kill other plants which are exposed to the spray, and in the pond it will be disastrous and kill all water life. Fruit-fall and collecting fruit cause further problems.

The rock garden is often a 'rockery' relegated to a corner under a tree with a pile of stones, and bits of concrete added as well. This simply will not work and prove a worthwhile rock garden. No soil is retained by the stones or concrete. It is too dry under the tree because water drips only on the outside area of the tree. The light is very poor as well.

Vegetables and soft fruit

Like the rock garden both these require good light, and in the re-arranged garden the vegetables have been retained. This area may also contain soft fruit such as strawberries, raspberries, currants etc. Vegetables and soft fruit never grow well near trees and shrubs, but some soft fruits will grow under shady walls and fences. This area would be better hidden from sight of the rock garden and house. This can be achieved by building either a retaining wall, if a sloping site exists as is shown, or raised beds, or both. Alternatively, a short screen of hedging or fencing can achieve the same objective, provided that neither the vegetable garden nor the raised areas are cast into shade.

Borders

The border shown in the original garden at the top of the diagram on page 4 is better removed altogether, whilst the border at the bottom is enlarged. This will allow shrubs and herbaceous plants to flourish and expand in a wider bed. The bed is no longer covered by trees in the re-designed garden. The light will be quite good provided that the plants do not grow too tall, and are graduated in size downwards from the back to front. The border can be entirely of shrubs, herbaceous or mixed plantings. The shrubs are easier to maintain but of course will have leaf-fall. The herbaceous plants, those which die down to ground level in the winter, will normally retain their leaves on the dead stems, and both are cut down in the winter and removed.

Bedding plants and annuals are best left to formal areas (below retaining walls for the best effect), but some can be grown for the front of a mixed border of shrubs and herbaceous plants.

Bog plants

These are herbaceous plants which grow in damp and wet places, but not actually in water. They associate well with alpines and rock plants, and if a naturally damp or wet place exists, then make use of it for these plants. If not, one can be created (see pages 40–43).

Pools

A large pool at the base of a rock garden will increase the appearance of all areas that surround it by reflection. Whether or not to have waterfall pools depends mainly on the size of the rock garden. Small ones that measure less than 10 sq yds (9 sq m) are better without any waterfall pools. See pages 24–25.

Climbers and roses

Hybrid tea and floribunda roses are formal in their planting and do not go well with informal structures like rock gardens and screes, but could be grown with the more formal raised beds and retaining walls. The reverse is true of old fashioned or shrub roses, which are informal in their planting and growth. Climbing roses and other climbing plants can be very effective on an otherwise harsh background of wall or fence. The size of the support and the volume of the climbers' leaf-fall will determine what is actually planted.

Lawns

Where the garden is large enough there is no doubt that a good lawn sets off the whole garden. However, a smaller garden, as illustrated here, can have a small area of grass which could be called a meadow. Bulbs can be grown in it and the grass is cut only between June and September; this allows the bulbs to die down naturally in uncut grass in spring and early summer. The grass will not be of top quality, but will show interesting changes throughout the year. See page 54.

The smallest gardens are better without any lawn at all, but can be paved instead, with plants growing between paving slabs to soften an otherwise harsh garden. Neither mowing machine nor shears are needed.

Here is the actual view of the rock garden shown in the ground plan on page 5. Although the overall area is small, careful design of the space has enabled a large range of plants to be grown under widely varying conditions. It includes sink gardens, a paved area which is planted, a raised bed, a pool with an adjacent bog garden, a scree, a tiny 'meadow' (the grassed area on the same terrace as the pool), and a rock garden at the higher levels. This gives the opportunity to grow plants which need perfect drainage, at one extreme, as well as those which require continuously wet conditions, at the other.

3. Equipment

The first step in planning the work of constructing a rock garden is to decide on the equipment that will be needed. For most people the job will not be sufficiently large to justify hiring mechanical diggers and the like, but nor will it be so small that operations cannot be made much easier by using the right tools. Some of these will be found in most garden sheds, some will be worth buying, some can be hired.

Stone work

For moving rocks into position, at least one crowbar measuring about 5 ft (1.5 m) is needed – larger for rocks weighing over 5 cwt (250 kg). It is easier, though, to use two crowbars for sizeable rocks. Where crowbars would be difficult or impossible to use, rope slings are best for moving the rocks – by placing slings under one end of the rock and moving the rock one end at a time.

Use a strong barrow to move smaller stones and rocks, but anything over 1 cwt (50 kg) requires a sack truck. Baulks of wood – ideally at least 3 in (7.5 cm) square at the ends – can be used as blocks under sack truck wheels to prevent the truck rolling prematurely when you are pulling back the handles after loading the stone, and these will also make good fulcrums for levering stones with crowbars.

Scaffold boards are essential for all construction work when wheelbarrows and sack trucks are involved – to give a smooth run over rough ground, to protect lawns, and for running a barrow up into a skip. Stone can be moved on scaffold boards by using rollers of up to 1 in (2.5 cm) steel rod (not piping), as illustrated on page 16. When using scaffold planks up unsupported slopes, it is advisable to place a support under the centre of each plank to prevent the planks whipping up and down.

Retaining walls, raised beds and screes, as well as rock gardens, require a club hammer weighing about 2 lbs (1 kg), a cold chisel about 1 in (2.5 cm) wide, and a bolster chisel about 4 in (10 cm) wide for chipping off unwanted pieces, splitting and shaping the rock. You will also need a spade for cutting out soil from the site, and a rammer for firming soil around stones already in position – a strong stake is ideal for this; do not rely on your feet for firming other than over large surface areas.

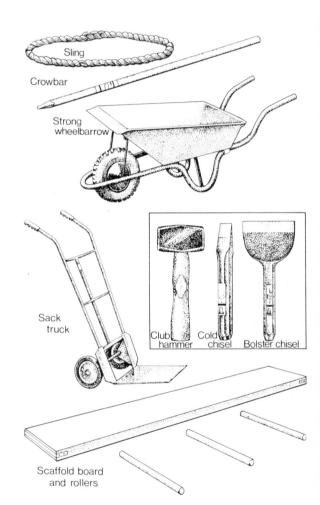

Sling

Crowbar

Strong wheelbarrow

Sack truck

Club hammer   Cold chisel   Bolster chisel

Scaffold board and rollers

Retaining walls

Where a retaining wall exceeds 15 ft (4.5 m) in length, two templates should be used to maintain the correct slope and keep a straight line. These can be rectangular pieces of plywood. They are prepared by placing them together and drilling holes through both at the angle required for the slope. When they are set up and levelled on the site, they should be anchored firmly, as shown in the

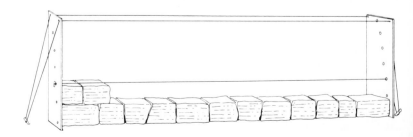

illustration, and string is then stretched across as work progresses upwards.

When the retaining wall is under 15 ft (4.5 m) in length, the corners should be built up at each end first so that wires can be inserted at intervals up each corner between the stones. Strings are then stretched between them as guidelines for laying the remaining stones.

Pools

Little equipment is needed for constructing pools with either a liner or glass-fibre mould – a spade, shovel, spirit level and a straight-edged board on which to place the spirit level. The board should be long enough, preferably, to run the length of the pool, but at the very least the width of it, and it must not bow when placed on its edge.

For liner pools made with concrete walls, you will need (apart from the materials which will actually make the concrete walls) sheets of hardboard to be used as shuttering. The standard sheet measures 8 ft × 4 ft (2.5 m × 1.2 m), which can be cut in two to give a 2 ft (60 cm) depth. You will also need stakes to hold the shuttering temporarily. A small bricklayer's trowel and wooden rammer are also essential.

The shuttering for concrete pools should be of 6 in × 1 in (15 cm × 2.5 cm) boards, held together by 2 in × 1 in (5 cm × 2.5 cm) battens. 3 in (7.5 cm) wire nails and 3 mm wire plus a claw hammer and pliers with wire cutters are also needed to fix the boards. Acrow jacks will hold the boards in position as the pool is built. A cement-mixer, electric or petrol-driven, is essential for large quantities of concrete, with a sheet of plastic underneath to save making a mess when loading and unloading.

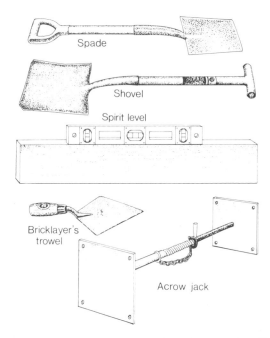

Spade

Shovel

Spirit level

Bricklayer's trowel

Acrow jack

Small tools like trowels and handforks are more suitable than large implements in rock gardens.

4. Preparation of the Site

Before you begin constructing your rock garden, you must ensure that it is clear of perennial weeds, has good drainage (unless you are contemplating a bog garden) and it must have a reasonably sunny and open aspect, free from close or overhanging trees and shrubs which are large enough to cause the kind of problems mentioned on pages 4–7.

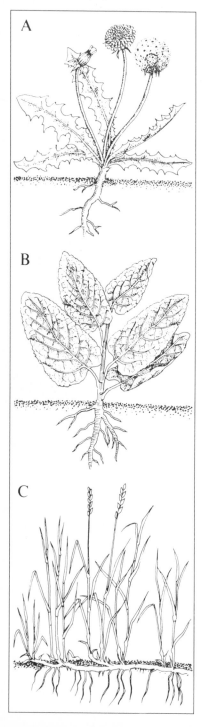

Perennial weeds

The perennial weeds are those which grow year after year from underground storage organs, which can appear as bulbs, underground or overground runners and tap roots, which are thickened rootstocks that go deep into the ground. The bulbs include *Allium* (onions) which are usually spread rapidly by seeds. Much worse are *Oxalis* species which come with pink and yellow, sometimes white flowers. Both of them are difficult to eradicate as there is no chemical control yet. They must be dug up together with the soil around them, and then either burnt or consigned to the dustbin. This should be done by July, before the bulbils which develop on the outside of each bulb have separated from the bulbs.

Dandelions (A), welsh poppies and docks (B) are tap-root forming, and can either be dug up or killed using a proprietary brand of glyphosate. (All other broad leaved plants will also be killed if sprayed.) If they are dug up, do take all the tap roots away, otherwise these will grow again.

Underground runners include couch grass (twitch) (C), bindweed (bellbine) (D), sorrel (E), stinging nettles (F) and ground elder. Couch grass can be removed by using a selective weedkiller specifically made for this – alloxydim-sodium, which is safe to use over most other plants without ill-effect. Other running weeds can be dug up or you can use glyphosate. Creeping buttercup can be treated in the same way as underground runners.

Unless these weeds are removed or killed before construction begins they can 'escape' under the structures and will be difficult to eradicate. Do follow manufacturers' instructions carefully.

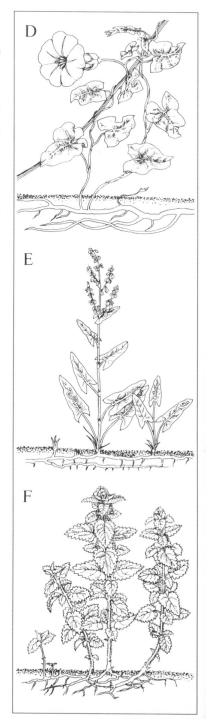

Drainage

The drainage for most gardens will be adequate on either the flat or sloping sites due to their raised designs. However, there are some situations where the drainage may be inadequate. The area which is paved over poorly drained soil will certainly need drainage. Where the underlying soil is of clay or similarly heavy soil, and the ground slopes down to the proposed rock garden, the water will have to be drained before it reaches the rock garden site. Where the site was originally flat and is now cut and filled the same drainage is needed.

The drains used are the 4 in (10 cm) diameter by 12 in (30 cm) long tiles which, if necessary, are easily cleaned with draining rods.

Where water is to be prevented from entering the site, sink the drains just below the surface by no more than 6 in (15 cm) and lay them directly onto firm soil. Then lay 1–2 in (3–5 cm) diameter gravel or similar stones to a depth of 4 in (10 cm) above and beside the tiles to allow water to seep into the drain. Do not put the gravel underneath the tiles, or the water will drain to the very site you are trying to prevent being soaked. Cover the stones with 2 in (5 cm) of well-drained soil.

A site which is partly below the normal ground level will require a drain silt trap to be laid at the lowest level and covered with a channel grating. The pit itself can be made of bricks with the drain tiles entering and leaving the pit at least 6 in (15 cm) above the base of the trap. The floor of the trap should be concreted to accommodate the bricks to be laid on it. This will give a good floor for cleaning the site out as well. Some of the lowest line of bricks have no mortar between them so that the water can escape by natural drainage. This allows any silt caught in the trap to be removed and saves using drain rods in the tiles. The drain must leave this low site for another equally low or lower one in order to drain away.

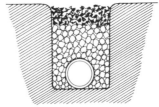

End section of drain, showing gravel laid at the sides and on top – to a depth of 4 in (10 cm) – to drain water into the 4 in (10 cm) tile. Soil that drains easily tops the gravel by 2 in (5 cm).

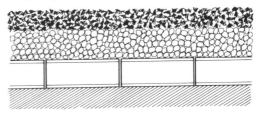

Side view of the same drain tiles 1 ft (30 cm) long, each butted up to one another.

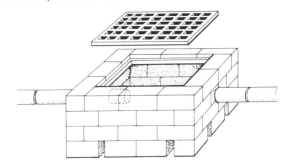

The silt trap for draining water from a low site, built of bricks. Gaps are left in the mortar at the lowest level to let the trap drain easily during dry periods and allow it to be cleaned. The drain tiles run into and out of the trap well above the base. A channel grating covers the trap.

Order of construction

Always build any structures from the base upwards. So, when building the garden on page 5, the first construction must be the pool, which is below ground; the second, a bog garden; the third the scree and the rock garden, or raised bed or retaining wall; fourth the paving; and last of all, the sink gardens. Where preparation and planting of the rest of the garden may be ruined by the construction work, leave them until all major work has been done – in our example the borders would be better planted after the pool, rock garden and steps are built. If this construction takes place in the autumn, there are no other major tasks like mowing and weeding to take up time. Hot work is obviously best carried out while the weather is cool.

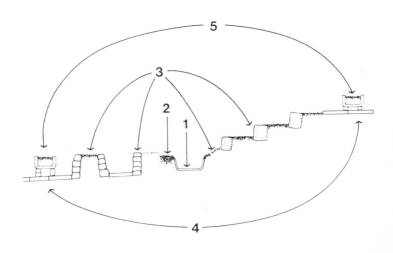

5. Stone Types

Stones or rocks come in a variety of types and sizes. Some are suitable for building rock gardens and screes, others for raised beds and retaining walls. Sites differ, and each has a prime type of stone to suit it, usually that of local origin.

Supply

Apart from the cost of quarrying and preparing the stone, transport is also expensive, and this must be borne in mind when choosing which type to buy. The stone can be bought direct from the quarries, or from local garden centres, or stone merchants. Usually the larger quantities will only be available direct from the quarry in the sizes specified for rock gardens. For screes, raised beds and retaining walls, the stone could be available locally as more random sizes can be used.

Do inspect the rocks you want so that you can pick out the individual ones required to do the job you intend to carry out, if it is a small one; or specify the sizes required. It causes much frustration and takes a great deal of effort to return them if they are found to be unsuitable when delivered!

Stone types

There are three basic types of rock available, only two of which are suitable for rock gardens and screes. The third is for raised beds and retaining walls. Rocks for sink gardens, stones for paved areas and tufa rock are considered separately on pages 36–37.

The first type, and the easiest to lay for rock gardens, is the sort which contains definite strata lines. Sandstone is one example; it is acid in reaction, and therefore suitable for all plantings, whether acid or lime-loving. The limestones with strata may be suitable for acid-lovers or not, according to whether they contain free lime in them. Ask the supplier. The strata lines are those which show how the rocks were laid down millons of years ago, layer upon layer, indicating the way they should be laid in the garden as well. (If laid the wrong way with the strata lines vertically arranged, frost action followed by thaws will eventually split the stone open and create problems.) There will also be crack lines running vertically which may mislead, but these are natural vents which show lines of upheaval stress. These vents are often used at the quarry to reduce the depths and lengths of rocks.

The second type of rock is formed by chemical action and water; an example is Westmorland limestone. This might not have any definite strata lines, but its shape dictates the way it is laid. These and some other rocks are very irregular in their outline, which makes them difficult to join together for rock gardens, but makes them ideal for screes (see page 34).

For raised beds and retaining walls, large and small stones can be mixed successfully, provided that they have relatively flat surfaces and are fairly regular in shape, so that one stone can be laid upon or beside another. No gaps should be left which could allow soil to slip through. Take care also when you make the construction that you lay the stones with the strata running horizontally, especially the top layer. A few can run vertically provided that they are not on the top layer, where they would be at risk of splitting (see

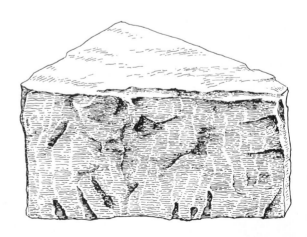

Westmorland limestone has an irregular shape with vertical and horizontal lines; it can be laid for a scree.

Ideal sandstone for joining easily to the next one at any point. The strata lines are horizontal and show the way it should be laid.

pages 30–35). Do not under any circumstances try to use granite, because it is metamorphic and lacks strata and character shape which help you build a successful structure. (Metamorphic rocks are the result of volcanic action, in which lava flows and cools to give no strata lines.)

Sizes

Stone is expensive, so make sure you are ordering what you want by reading the relevant chapters on each form of rock laying before deciding. For rock gardens and screes, use the largest sizes of height or length that can be handled successfully. In rock gardens it is not normally necessary to have a great depth from front to back as this adds to the cost. Rocks with great depth are of no value, except for the keystones which are explained on pages 18 and 22. The shorter the height of the rock, the greater should be its length to ensure stability. No hard and fast rules can apply about manageable weights, but rocks up to 4 cwt (200 kg) can be safely handled by two able-bodied people. Rocks of greater weight require three or four people. But a great deal depends on technique rather than muscle power, and teamwork is essential to avoid accidents. Do not rush the work otherwise errors and aching backs will be the result. It is not a fast job, but it is a very satisfying and rewarding one.

The stone for walls of raised beds and retaining walls can be of various sizes, and can be of manufactured materials which will be uniform in size (see pages 26–31). Never mix the stone types nor manufactured materials, or the result will look very odd.

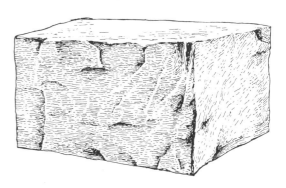

A sandstone of rectangular shape easily fitted into a line of stones.

Slate of thin texture as shown here, but often thicker, is ideal for screes when angled into the ground.

Topping materials

For rock gardens, and screes in particular, a material which matches the type of rock used is laid on the top 4 in (10 cm) to give perfect drainage at ground level. This can be of gravel, or limestone chippings, or broken rock of the same type. Even granite chippings can be used if the rocks have the same appearance as granite. The size of chippings depends on the size of site and size of rocks used. Generally, chippings measure between $\frac{3}{4}$ in (1.5 cm) and 2 in (5 cm) in diameter. Larger stones can be used, but it is inadvisable to use smaller, for they will not serve the purposes of attractive appearance and good drainage.

An imposing series of terraces is formed by massive rocks on a sloping site.

6. Soils

Gardens have such a mixture of soil types and a variety of capabilities. Some will be suitable as they are for alpines and rock plants, where the drainage is good, and the soil is of a good loam for good quality plants without further addition. But these gardens are rare, and most will need additional material added to the top layer to ensure that both drainage and water retention are balanced, with enough nutrient in the soil to maintain them for many years.

Soils have various sizes of grains, from very fine grains in clay soils; larger grains and humus in loam, this being a very good soil which is neither clay nor sandy and used for most purposes; to sandy, gritty and stony ones up the scale to gravel. Most soils have a mixture of these. Chalk soils have very quick drainage and little humus, which is fine for some plants, but not all. Some soils have a high lime content. Those which are acid in reaction are generally sand, with often a high humus content.

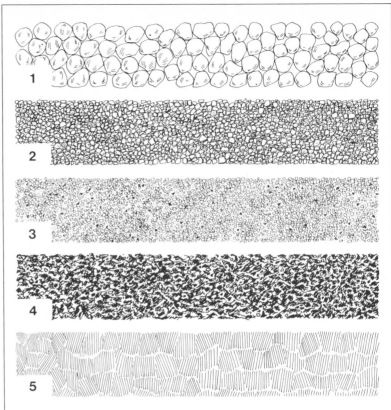

1. Shingle of ⅝in (1.5 cm) grains can be of any material; this is the smallest size recommended for topping material. 2. Grit with smaller grains, feels rough when rubbed in the hands. 3. Sand with easily seen grains, and soft feel when rubbed in the hands. 4. Loam with humus and fine particles. 5. Clay with very fine particles.

Soils for alpines and rock plants

These plants require good drainage, with provision for plenty of water in the spring and early summer when they are in growth. In their natural habitat most of them are under snow during the winter months which keeps them from drying out, but they are also free from atmospheric moisture, and the cold, wet conditions which prevail in most of the British Isles and other moist northern climates. It follows therefore, that the amount of drainage the plants demand depends on the area where the garden is situated.

In the interests of good drainage, extra grit and peat can be added to soils such as the John Innes composts, which are generally available. John Innes No 2 mix is ideal for planting purposes. This has 7 parts loam, 3 parts peat and 2 parts sand. You can have up to 4 more parts of peat and 5 extra parts of grit rather than sand. All these parts are by bulk and no further fertiliser need be added, which is why John Innes No 2 is recommended for rock garden plants at planting time. Grit is the material which has a coarse feel when rubbed in the hands, and the grains measure up to ⅛ in (3 mm) in diameter. It is unlike sand which feels soft when rubbed together.

Soils can vary, with perhaps extra peat but not so

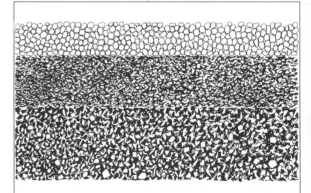

Three levels of soil in an alpine bed. The bottom layer is the garden top soil. The middle layer is the introduced soil of equal parts by bulk of loam, peat and grit, and is at least 6 in (15 cm) deep; it can be topped in any construction by the third layer of shingle or similar material to match the stone or rock used. It is essential for the scree and must be 4 in (10 cm) deep. It is optional for other sites.

much grit in East Anglia; the opposite in the north west of England and north Wales and most of Scotland. It all depends on the rainfall in the area. Scotland varies even more because of the difference between west and east coast temperature, and north compared to south, but alpines grow well in colder areas, because that is where most of them come from.

Feeding

Alpines do not need a very rich diet as this will make them grow too fast. On the other hand they do not do well on a poor one. The potash-based fertilisers will help to give controlled growth with plenty of flowers and, where applicable, fruits. The idea, which unfortunately is common, that they do best on a starvation diet is simply not true. It is the often harsh climate that is harder to emulate, and a sun-trapped area between walls will require plenty of water in dry weather to compensate for the water loss, and therefore feeding will be more necessary because fertilisers will be washed out. This is also true of wet areas of the country where temperatures do not often go very low in winter, and growth hardly stops. Feeding should take place each year in early spring. For colder and drier areas feeding could be as little as once every three years and this is achieved by a mixture of potash-based fertilisers and bonemeal at the rate of 1 oz per square yard of equal parts of the two fertilisers. Once every two years should be enough for other parts of the country.

Soil for bog plants

This is more difficult to control; if the soil is next to water, then liquid or solid fertilisers applied to the surface of the bog garden will also supply the water with feed. When this happens algal growth increases. So feed underneath the soil surface and below most root levels, which is at least 6 in (15 cm) below the soil, when planting and replanting. This could be done at least once every five years but preferably every three years, when dividing the plants.

Acid or alkaline

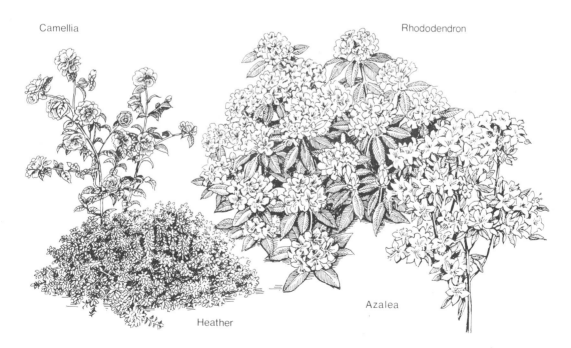

Acid soils are those in which plants such as rhododendrons, azaleas, camellias and heathers thrive. Alkaline or limy soils will not allow these plants to grow well. It is not always safe to apply this rule of thumb, however, to gardens by the sea, for in these areas such plants can fail because of the salt spray, rather than because of their intolerance of the soil.

7. Rock Garden Construction – Sloping Site

The purpose of any rock garden construction is to grow plants. The more natural it looks and uncomplicated in design or construction, the better the plants will look. Any construction should form a series of flat, horizontal terraces, each of which is able to retain soil without movement. Good drainage can be assured, especially nearest the edge of a drop to the lower level, by soil introduced to satisfy just this requirement. A means of watering will need to be provided, particularly in the early stages of growth, or in very dry conditions. And access is necessary to enable this to be undertaken, along with planting, weeding, top dressing and feeding, so terraces must be built with these operations in mind. Do not space the terraces too far apart so that you are continually treading on the soil when working. Instead, build a scree if this is likely to be the case (see pages 20–21).

Marking out and estimating

The site can be marked out with ropes or thick string to show the lines to be followed. 'Bend' the ends into the slope to allow them to 'disappear' and prevent erosion of the soil on the corners. If a flight of steps is required, as shown in the example garden on page 5, then incorporate these in the bend of the rock garden and mark them out at the same time. By marking out the site in this way, the length of stone required can be measured as well as its height. In the garden illustrated, the tops of the highest line of stone will be level with the path above.

To measure the height of each layer of stones, measure the difference in height between each level as marked out and add 1 inch (2.5 cm), which is the depth for the rocks to be set into the ground. The end rocks may be shorter in some instances where the layer bends into the slope. Repeat this measuring for each layer. In this way, the length and height of each layer of stones can be worked out.

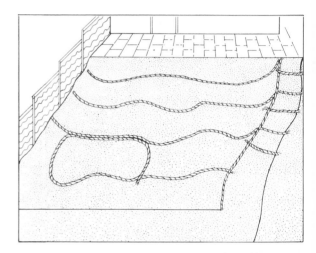

The site marked out with ropes to show where each terrace of rock will be laid, including the steps on the right-hand side.

Moving the rocks

Rock can be ordered from a garden centre or direct from a quarry, but do inspect it first, and be careful not to shatter any by having it carelessly tipped out of a lorry when it arrives.

When the rock can be delivered directly into the garden where it is to be used, a sack truck is suitable for moving blocks up to 4 cwt (200 kg) in weight to the point where they are to be laid. They can, alternatively, be moved by using a crowbar and a baulk of wood as a fulcrum, turning the rock end over end to the final position. When a block is heavier than 4 cwt (200 kg) use the crowbar and a fulcrum to move first one end, then the other, by a rolling action on the crowbar. Where the ground is firm this will be relatively easy, but on softer ground use scaffold planks over the ground to prevent your apparatus sinking into the earth.

Where the rock is to be moved over concrete or paving (as you may have to when moving it from the front garden to the back garden), don't tip the rock end over end; this might damage both it and the paving. Use the sack truck or, if the weight is too heavy, use a pair of planks placed side by side. Lay solid steel rollers – parallel to each other and at right angles to the planks – on top of these, and then more planks on top of the rollers. Place wedges between the two sets of planks at each end to prevent them moving too soon.

Next to the planks and rollers position some baulks of wood so that their tops are level with the top of the planks; ease the rock onto the baulks, and then shift it one end at a time onto the planks. If the rock is

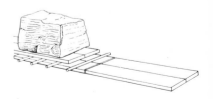

A rock mounted on one pair of parallel planks. Four solid steel rollers are sandwiched between two sets of planks, wih another set forward. The rock is pushed or crowbared along with ease.

not resting on this platform of wood, you will find that the top planks will tip over as soon as you move the rock onto them. Ease the rock into the centre of the planks, even out the ground over which the boards are to be placed, then take out the wedges.

The rollers should, of course, be immediately under the rock and at least one forward of it. The rock moves forward, either pushed by hand, or eased with a crowbar below one of the upper planks in short upward and forward movements. Take out the rear rollers, and place them forward as the rock moves forward. Use the crowbars to lift the upper planks gently if placing the forward roller is difficult.

As the end of the lower planks is reached, place two more planks forward and butt them to the original ones. Be careful not to jam a roller between the two sets of planks as it moves forward. To turn corners, place the forward set of planks at an angle of not more than 20° to the rear pair at a time. As the rock reaches the angle, let it run slightly over the forward pair of planks. Then crowbar the rock over towards the line of the forward pair; move further forward, then repeat the process until the line of the rock is straight to the lower planks.

Do not wait until you reach the passage at the side of a house before turning, as there will not be enough room to adjust the angle.

When the site is reached and if the rock is more easily rolled downhill, use the baulks of wood at the bottom to prevent it rolling too far at the point it is required.

If the site is uphill from the passage, the rock will be best eased forward one end at a time off the rollered planks and up the hill on one set of planks without rollers. Never use the planks and rollers method uphill, as both planks and rocks will simply roll back.

When you need to cross over grass always use scaffold planks to prevent damage to the grass, even when using a sack truck.

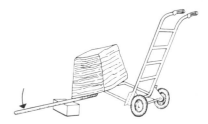

To get a rock up to 4 cwt (200 kg) in weight onto a sack truck, lift one end of the rock using a baulk of wood as a fulcrum, and push the sack truck under the rock.

Use the crowbar and baulk of wood to lift the rock, and pull back on the handles of the sack truck with blocked wheels at the same time; this lifts the rock into the moving position.

This sloping site has been terraced with a series of retaining walls (see pages 30–31) rather than the lines of massive rocks described here. Lines of rocks receding into the slope give the impression of natural strata, as can be seen in the photographs on pages 13 and 21.

Laying the rocks

Always lay the rocks from the base level upwards, never the other way round as the bottom layer always ends up being buried too deeply. Any hose-pipe that is needed for a waterfall should be laid before the rocks (see page 20).

1. Remove the soil along the lines you have laid out to a depth of 1 inch (2.5 cm) to accommodate the rocks you have chosen. Don't remove too much soil; if you have to put some back you will then have a soft base for the rocks, which will cause them to settle and your line will become ragged.

2. Choose one of the largest rocks as a keystone to be laid more or less centrally on the bottom level, as illustrated. The keystone is ideally wider at the front than at the back, so that it makes a firm wedge in the terrace. In the diagram it is set just over the edge of a pond, tilting back slightly to give greater stability. Use one or two crowbars and baulks of wood to ease the stone into position; a spade can be used as a skid underneath. Always use the crowbars far more than your back when moving rocks, and get others to help you. When working as a team be careful that each member of the team knows what the others are going to do before any move is made.

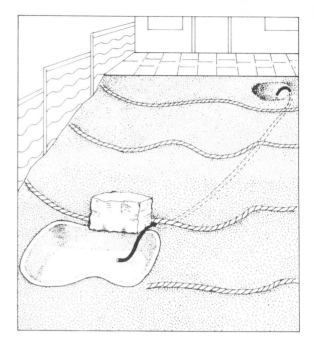

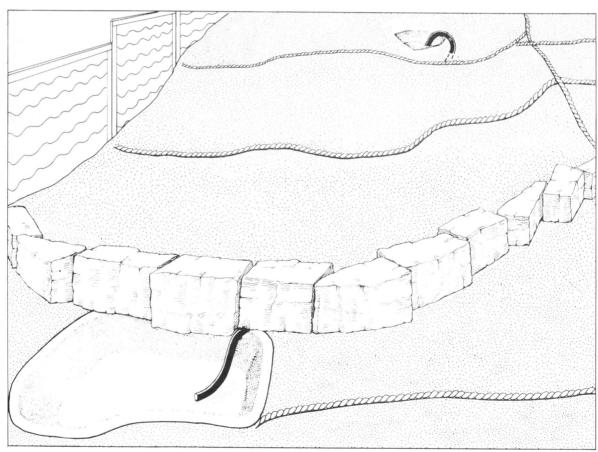

When the pool is in position (see page 24), the first line of rocks can be laid.

3. Rocks may vary in height, so match them up before laying the rest by measuring them. Having laid one rock locked in on one side of the keystone (leaning back into the slope, as the keystone does, for stability), make sure that you continue to lock the stones into the chain with the keystone as the central wedge. Do not change the overall direction of the line, or else the construction will be weak. Most rocks will have to be shaped with a club hammer and cold chisel or bolster. Hold the chisel at an angle of at least 45° to the piece of rock to be chipped off. Hit it firmly, but not too heavily to begin with, then more firmly as it begins to chip off, and lower the angle of the chisel.

4. The tops of each line of rocks should be level, with no spaces that would allow soil to slip away. Neither the tops nor the sides should leak soil, but if you cannot match up rocks without gaps, then odd pieces can be inserted, but they must be firmly wedged behind the larger rocks.

5. Fill in behind the line of rocks with garden soil to keep it stable. (Some of this soil will be scooped out later and replaced with a suitable planting medium, as described over the page.) When soil is filled in behind, the back tops of the rocks are not seen (remember that the rocks are leaning into the slope) and this gives the impression that the rocks go back in a continuous seam.

6. The second and subsequent layers are laid in exactly the same way, with rocks laid from the keystone outwards. Set each line of stones 1 in (2.5 cm) below the top of the lower layer of rocks; as with the first layer, this gives more stability but also prevents soil being eroded from underneath the stones. If you have to lift the rocks up the slope to the next layer, use a sack truck to do this by placing the handles of the truck on the bottom layer and levering the rock onto the truck and then over the handles, as shown in the illustration. Alternatively, slide one side of the rock up the truck and then the other, a short distance at a time. Mind your fingers in either case.

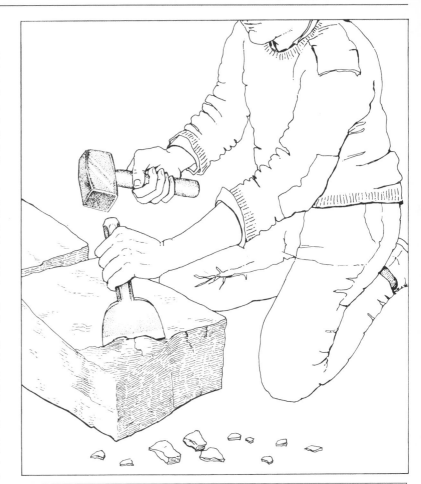

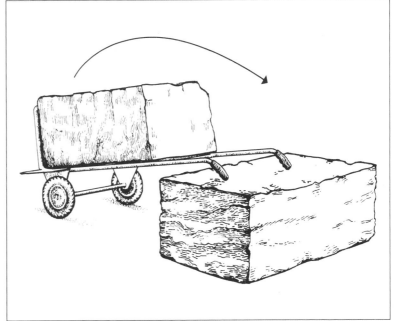

To lay the rock in an uphill position, place the handles of the sack truck to rest on the first layer of rock. The rock is then rolled end over end, or eased one side at a time a short distance towards the handles. This makes off-loading much easier.

Waterfalls

If ponds for waterfalls are to be incorporated, do make sure that at each proposed outlet point either a channel can be chipped out of one rock, or be chipped out of two adjoining rocks where they may be less deep from front to back.

To ensure a watertight seal between each pool, a continuous length of liner can be laid from top to bottom including each waterfall pool. This means that the hosepipe through which the water is pumped from the base pool to the top has to be laid before any rocks. The liner for each waterfall pool must be laid before the rocks above it are laid. By installing this continuous run of liner, you ensure that any water lost behind a stone will run into the next pool.

The alternative method is to use fibreglass waterfalls with sufficient overlap between each to prevent water loss. The fibreglass pools should also be laid when building the rock garden to ensure a neat fit, so that any adjustments can be made at the time to the pools and rocks together.

It is possible to use concrete for this purpose, but it is quite complex and not recommended unless larger waterfall pools are required. It is not intended that any planting should be made in any of the waterfall pools; they supply the sound and movement in small volume from a submersible pump into the much larger base pond, where the plants are grown, and fish and other water life also appear.

The electric cable should be laid after the rock garden is constructed and, in the case of the rock garden illustrated, before the steps are laid. Get professional advice before attempting this.

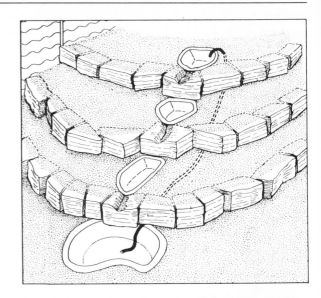

The relative positions of hosepipe (dotted line), the three waterfall pools (centre of each terrace), and the rocks laid in each terrace before the steps are laid.

Steps

The steps are laid, preferably with a minimum of two steps to each terrace in the rock garden. Each end 'disappears' into the rock garden on one side and into the border on the other side. The steps will be safe without a rail for support as long as the rock steps are placed so that there is at least 2½ times the depth of tread for each single step up.

The area behind each step can be of rock or soil. The rocks will need to be at least 1 ft (30 cm) deep to be stable. Soil is perfectly satisfactory provided that it is level with the tops of the steps. If the soil is sticky, add chippings to match the rocks used, and press these into the top soil.

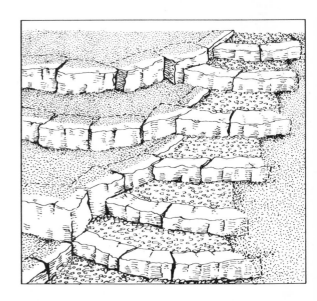

The completed steps. The depth of each tread should be at least two and a half times the height of each rise.

Soil and top dressings

On completion of the construction, take out at least 6 in (15 cm) but preferably 9 in (23 cm) of soil in each terrace, and replace it with a soil mix as recommended on pages 14–15. Where vertical plantings are wanted between rocks, these will have to be carried out during construction (see pages 32–33).

The soil depth on each terrace should cover the back tops of every rock to give the impression that the rocks go on into the slope, just as on a rocky coastline.

If it is wished, a topping material can be given to the soil. Topping materials are mentioned on page 35 and are as for screes, but lay them to a depth of only 1 in (2.5 cm). This will give a clean and natural appearance, but would be most easily laid after planting. Maintenance of the completed rock garden will also be simpler.

This rock garden on a sloping site has a waterfall flowing into the pool beneath. *Dodecatheon media* is in the foreground, *Pulsatilla vulgaris* is to the right, and *Arenaria balearica* has covered the north-facing aspect of the rocks within three years of planting. The dwarf, deep pink shrub on the rocks to the right is *Daphne cneorum* 'Eximea'.

8. Rock Garden Construction – Flat Site

Most gardens will be on a flat or almost flat site, and the construction of a rock garden for these gardens has to be different in its approach. The most important factor is that it can be built anywhere in the garden, so long as it is accessible from all round, with no part touching a fence or dividing-wall during or on completion of construction, otherwise damage can occur to fence and walls. The result of this kind of open positioning is that all aspects of north, east, south and west must be taken into consideration. In practice, one or more of these aspects can be enlarged and others reduced. To gain the greatest advantage it would be best to enlarge the southern and western aspects, and reduce the eastern and northern ones.

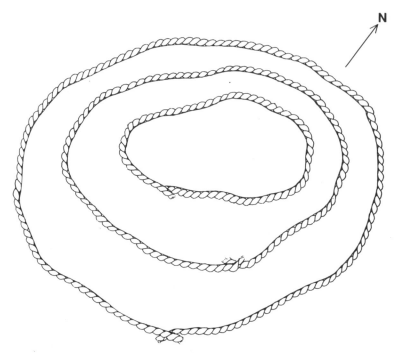

A flat site marked out with rope. On the north side the planting area has been reduced, whilst the south, east and west have been enlarged to allow more plantings in sunny positions.

Design

Lay the ropes out to form each line of stone, but raise the inner ones on canes to the appropriate heights to give an indication of how it will look. Bear in mind the depth of stone in each layer from front to back, and allow for this when estimating the number of layers, required. The design is much better if kept simple and, normally, confined to a maximum height of three layers. Avoid fussy top-knots of stone; they do not look good, and are expensive. The build-up of more height will come by planting, but do not have tall plants on top, as they will look artificial.

Simple flat site

Lay the rocks in the same way as for a sloping site, from the base upwards, starting with a keystone, and lean all the rocks inwards. But, because it is a flat site, all the rocks will have to be laid using a spirit level all the way round. Otherwise the rocks finishing on

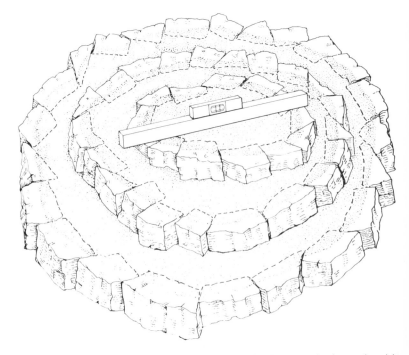

The three layers have been laid according to the lines marked out. A spirit-level is used to maintain a constant top level on each layer of rocks.

the opposite side will not match up and this will result in erosion from the taller side. Quite apart from this, it will look very odd to have uneven tops to all the rocks. This makes it more difficult to lay, of course, than on the sloping site but, in compensation, because the site is flat there are no slopes to cope with.

Cut and fill

The more complex method of dealing with a flat site is by a process of cut and fill. Soil is removed from part of the site, and heaped onto an adjacent part. This can be done more than once on the same site, and a perfect example of this is to be seen at the Royal Botanic Gardens, Kew, Richmond in Surrey.

The top soil is removed first (the darker soil) from the whole site; then the sub-soil is dug from the 'cut' area, and placed on the area to be raised. The sides of both cut and fill are sloped to not more than a 45° angle, but it can be less. The greater the angle the more stone is used. The top soil is replaced over the whole area. The rocks are laid preferably after three months to allow the soil to settle, or longer if you can wait (the more settled the better). It will help to tread down each 6 in (15 cm) layer laid of sub- and top soil.

The base layers of rock are laid starting at least 1 in (2.5 cm) below ground level, and the bases of the subsequent layers are laid just below the tops of the previous layers. This gives stability and prevents erosion of soil from under the rocks. Base soil can be any reasonable garden soil; the top 6–9 in (15–23 cm) will be as recommended on pages 14–15.

Cut and fill

Top soil is removed from the whole area.

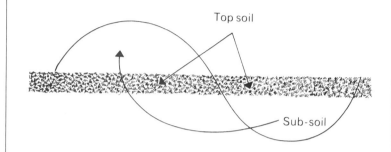

Top soil

Sub-soil

The sub-soil from the 'cut' area is formed into a mound.

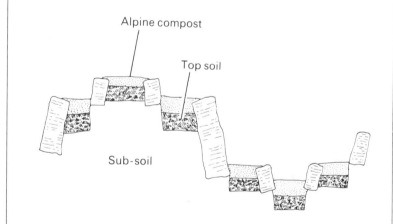

Alpine compost

Top soil

Sub-soil

A cross-section of the completed 'cut and fill' rock garden. The top soil has been replaced and then a layer of alpine soil (see page 14) has been firmed down on top of that.

Drainage

In order to ensure good drainage, do make sure that the lowest level is above the water table, otherwise it will end up as a water or bog garden! The water table is the level to which water normally rises in the ground, and for the purpose of building a rock garden, you should allow for the level it could rise to under flood conditions.

Drains laid in clay or heavy soils need to be placed at a level below the lowest point of the rock garden to an exit point which is lower than the starting point. A fall of 1 in 200 is all that is necessary, and an open end to the drain will need to be kept clean at the exit. Lay gravel on the top and sides of the drains to a depth of 4 in (10 cm) before replacing the soil (see page 11). For sandy soils this will not normally be necessary if drainage is otherwise perfectly adequate.

9. Pools

The most effective position for a pool in the rock garden is at the foot, because it makes the construction look bigger by reflecting it in the water. Most of the pools built are too small, so it is worth outlining not only the area of the pool but also the spread of plants within it to see if what you plan will be large enough. Waterfall pools and waterfalls are more complicated additions, but the sound of water splashing, and the sight of it in motion can give great pleasure. These can be designed as simple containers to hold water which splashes down to the next level (see page 20); the planting is then reserved entirely for the base pool.

Pool liners

There are three possible ways to build a pool. The first method is to use a liner, but when a rock garden rises steeply above it, the soil must be of clay or similar density to prevent the weight of the rocks pushing the soil down onto the liner.

Choose a liner made of butyl, which can have a life of fifty years or more. PVC with reinforcing has an approximate life of ten to fifteen years; PVC without reinforcing a life of about ten years.

Dig out the soil to a minimum depth of 20 in (50 cm), but preferably 24–30 in (60–75 cm), with sloping sides all the way round at an angle of about 110° to the base. A marginal planting shelf should be incorporated that is 6–9 in (15–23 cm) wide and also 6–9 in below the proposed water level. The shelf can go all or part of the way round the pool, but must be cut at the same 110° angle as the rest of the pool; the purpose of this slope is to prevent the soil caving in when the liner is laid.

Remove all sharp objects and lay soft sand over the whole area to be covered by the liner; the walls can be protected by thick wads of damp newspaper (see the illustration of a cross-section). You can calculate the size of liner required by this formula: (twice the depth + length + 2 overlaps) × (twice the depth + breadth + 2 overlaps). The overlap is an area of at least 6 in (15 cm) beyond the edges of the pool, and is necessary for anchoring the liner; the other dimensions must be measured at the maximum points of your excavation. Lay the liner over the site, allowing the overlaps, and fill the cavity with water, whereupon the liner will take on the shape of the pool.

Cover the edges with whatever surrounds the pool – lawn, scree, slabs etc. The liner should ideally be hidden so that ultra-violet light does not damage it; it is, therefore, very important that the level should be even all the way round.

A liner pool can be constructed with vertical sides to enable you to place planting baskets close to the edge by building concrete walls. Cut hardboard sheets of standard 8 × 4 ft (2.4 m × 1.2 m) size to give two sheets each 8 × 2 ft (2.4 m × 60 cm); it is best to paint these with limewash to prevent them sticking to the concrete. Dig the pool 2 ft (60 cm) deep, with upright sides, and fix the hardboard to stakes around the inside of the pool, leaving a 3 in (7.5 cm) gap between the hardboard and the soil wall. Drive $\frac{1}{2}$ in (1.5 cm) steel rods, 3 ft (90 cm) apart, to act as reinforcing. Pour in a concrete mix by bulk of 1 part cement to 12 parts of $\frac{5}{8}$ in (1.5 cm) aggregate to a consistency of toothpaste when water is added. Tamp down well every 6 in (15 cm) layer all the way round, and replace the soil removed from the pool to balance up the pressure on the shuttering. When the top is reached, check the level all the way round and smooth the concrete.

Remove the soil and shuttering four days later, and rub off any sharp edges of concrete with a brick or similar object. Lay fibreglass matting underlay, which is obtainable from butyl suppliers, over all the concrete surface, remove sharp objects and lay sand on the floor. Lay the liner as suggested above. The illustration shows a cross-section of the completed pool, with the overlap of the liner turned down so that turf can be laid to the edge of the pool.

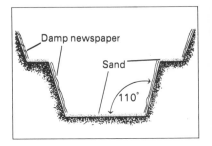

Cross-section of an excavation prepared for a pool liner.

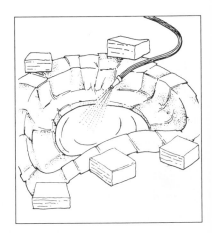

Water being added to the pool once the liner is in position and its overlaps weighted down.

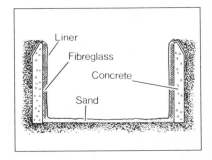

Cross-section of a liner pool with concrete sides.

Fibreglass pools

The second method of building a pool is with a pre-formed fibreglass pool, whose shape and size (generally quite small) are determined by the manufacturer. Don't try to dig a hole to the same shape as the pool you have bought, but excavate one appreciably larger; it should be large enough for you to fill around the pool with ease. Remove any sharp objects, place sand over the whole site and then insert the pool into the hole. Use bricks to support it as you get it level, and ensure that its top is an inch or so below ground level; filling in around the pool is bound to raise it a little and bring it up flush with the ground. Add water at the same time as you fill in around it to give stability.

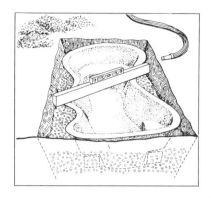

Concrete pools

A concrete pool is quite an ambitious undertaking. The procedure is similar to that for building a liner pool with concrete sides, but the shuttering cannot be supported on stakes driven into the floor of the pool, so you must use acrow jacks (see page 9). Also, the concrete must be thicker and waterproof.

It is possible to avoid shuttering by building the pool with sloping sides, as shown here. The purpose of the polythene is to prevent the concrete drying out too quickly, which might cause hair cracks to form. After a 4 in (10 cm) layer of concrete (to which a waterproofing agent has been added) has been laid over the whole site, large mesh wire is pressed into it and then a further 2 in (5 cm) of concrete covers that. The concrete must set slowly to prevent cracks, so cover it with wet sacking or some similar material. After about a week, seal the concrete with a suitable sealant, available from garden centres, to prevent lime escaping from the concrete and polluting the water.

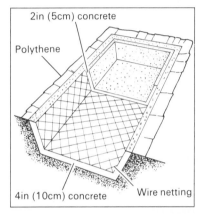

2in (5cm) concrete

Polythene

4in (10cm) concrete

Wire netting

A pool does not need to be placed in a confined area. Here, distant views enhance its effect.

10. Raised Beds

Raised beds have many advantages. All are free-standing and can be reached from all sides. As most gardens are on a flat site, they can be built more easily than can a rock garden on the same site, especially where space is limited. Limited space also often means less light; a bed raised 3 ft (90 cm) will gain more of this. Raised beds have all aspects, north, east, south and west, are easy to manage once built, and are ideal for the disabled and elderly. They can be used as short barriers against areas which the owner does not wish to see from the house. The existing garden soil is irrelevant, as soil can be introduced to suit alpines. And, finally, drainage is not a problem.

Designs

The shape could be formal as this makes construction easier and gives a good finish. It can be rectangular, a curved rectangle, L-shaped or circular.

The height depends upon who is to maintain it, what is to be grown in it, and what the soil is like underneath it. It also depends on whether the structure will be used as a seat. The minimum height for the bed to make its presence felt is 1 ft (30 cm) above the surrounding ground. The maximum is 3 ft (90 cm), because a greater height would not be in proportion with the width.

Low designs can have stepping stones placed flush with the soil for stepping onto the site and the design can be wide, up to about 8 ft (2.4 m). When built between 1½–2 ft (45–60 cm) high, then width should be reduced to 5 ft (1.5 m), because stepping onto the raised bed is difficult, and an average person's reach is limited to about 2½ ft (75 cm) from each side to the centre. From 2–3 ft (60–90 cm) high, the width can increase for able-bodied people to 6 ft (1.8 m), because the knees and thighs can rest against the structure so that you can bend forward and increase your reach considerably. The elderly and disabled should only have to reach a maximum of 2 ft (60 cm) from each side. Those in wheelchairs should ideally have raised beds 2 ft (60 cm) high by 4 ft (1.2 m) wide to enable them to work on the structure. The width of any site should not be less than 3 ft (90 cm), as it would be liable to dry out too quickly and need frequent watering.

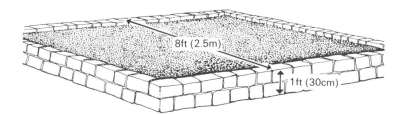

A low design can be stepped across, and can therefore be wide.

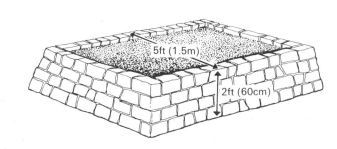

A design of medium height restricts the width to your maximum reach from each side.

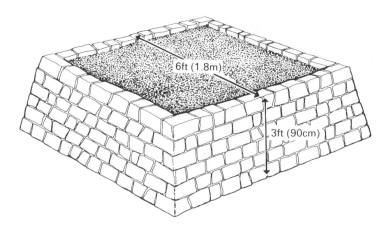

A slightly higher design can be wider as you can support yourself against it and lean across.

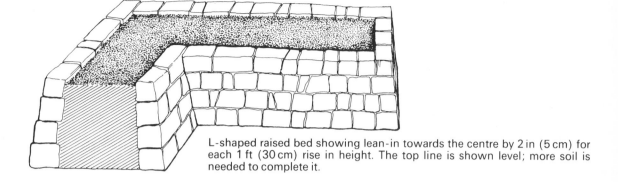

L-shaped raised bed showing lean-in towards the centre by 2 in (5 cm) for each 1 ft (30 cm) rise in height. The top line is shown level; more soil is needed to complete it.

Rectangular raised bed with soil also not high enough to cover the back top of every stone. The site is sloping and shows how the lowest stones are staggered in the ground.

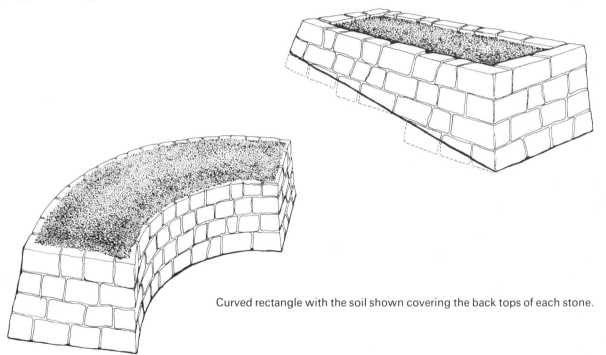

Curved rectangle with the soil shown covering the back tops of each stone.

Materials

The range of materials is large. Railway sleepers are the easiest to erect, but be careful in warm weather when the tar may become sticky and get onto clothing and hands. Natural stone is of course ideal, and usually supplied by the square yard or square metre of the face; the face is the part of the stone which faces outwards when laid. Stones can be supplied in sizes from thin 'slates' to large cubes. Do use one type of stone only for each raised bed; for example, Sussex sandstone, or Cheddar stone, not the two together.

Various manufactured walling stones which are of uniform size, and bricks, can be used. For heights up to 2 ft (60 cm) they can be laid without mortar between them. Above this height they are better mortared together.

Building blocks of various sizes made of concrete can be used. They are stark and would need vigorous-growing plants to trail from the top to hide them (see pages 46–47). They can be mortared together but this may not be necessary because they are larger than the bricks and manufactured stones, and therefore more stable if they are laid on their largest surface areas.

Mortared raised beds

These will be upright when laid, allowing for $\frac{1}{2}$ in (1.3 cm) of mortar between each block vertically and horizontally. They should have 6–9 in (15–23 cm) of concrete footings beneath them, using 12 parts by bulk of $\frac{5}{8}$ in (1.5 cm) aggregate, to 1 part by bulk of cement. The 6 in (15 cm) depth is for heavy soils, and 9 in (23 cm) for light soils, to support walls up to 3 ft (90 cm) high. Use a strong mortar mix between the blocks of 3 parts by bulk of builder's sand to 1 part of cement.

Mortared structure materials will be bricks, manufactured stones and concrete blocks. All except the concrete blocks can be shaped (into a shape similar to that shown in the illustration of railway sleepers opposite) with a club hammer and bolster chisel to allow plantings to be made in the walls. It is advisable not to attempt to shape concrete blocks at all, as they are difficult to cut accurately.

Dry-stone raised beds

These offer more potential than mortared ones, and they can be built as time permits, without those limitations that must be taken into account when using mortar mixes. They also look more natural in the garden. They do not have concrete footings, but are started just below ground level for stability. A batter (backwards slope) of approximately 2 in (5 cm) for each 1 ft (30 cm) rise in height is advisable to maintain the stability. Lay them with no two joints overlapping vertically which would weaken the structure. There should be no gaps between the stones which could allow soil to run out, except at points where plants are wanted.

It is easier if the corners are built up first, if in fact there are corners. Some of the larger pieces can be used for corner stones, and the lines for the remainder can be followed by eye. There is no need for exact lines, as long as the raised bed is stable.

A simple raised bed of irregular design. If it were a regular shape, it would hold more plants without taking up more space.

Railway sleepers

Railway sleepers can be laid as shown in the diagram, or they could be laid any height up to 3 ft (90 cm). Some of them will have to be cut in half. As they measure 8 ft (2.4 m) long, it is easier to plant the construction in the raised bed in multiples of 8 ft (2.4 m). This will reduce the wastage to nothing, especially if the width is kept to 4 ft (1.2 m) as well. To make places for planting with very little extra cutting, but a slight increase in overall length, cut some of the sleepers at a 70° angle when cutting them in half. Turn over one half to give a V-shaped opening inside the raised bed. Where they are to lie together, carve out with a sharp knife or chisel a hole, half from each side, about 1 in (2.5 cm) in diameter. This will allow enough room for the neck of any plant to rest in it, with the roots inside, and head outside.

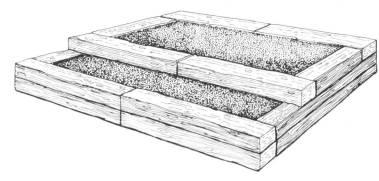

Railway sleepers used as a double deck raised bed. Whole sleepers are used for the length of the site. Sleepers cut to half their length used for the ends, and the top ends are quarter the length. Shown with the soil level not yet high enough.

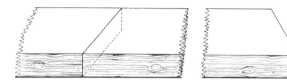

Making a plant-hole. The principle is the same in stone-work.

Soil and planting

Any unmortared structure built above 1 ft (30 cm) high must have the soil put inside the structure at the same time as the wall is built. It should be well trodden down every 6 in (15 cm) in depth. For the planting in the side walls, the soil should be as recommended on pages 14–15 and fill up that area extending 9 in (22 cm) behind the wall. It should also be used for a top layer to the same depth. The remaining soil can be any reasonable earth available, provided that it is free from perennial weeds. The soil should be at least 1 in (2.5 cm) higher than the wall top to allow for settling, and to cover the backs of the stones. Sub-soil can be used for beds deeper than 2 ft (60 cm).

Planting must be done during construction between the raised bed materials. Never try to force roots into gaps afterwards. It is safer to plant too many and remove afterwards any surplus plants, than to damage them by planting later to replace any that may have died. This applies also to preformed holes in mortared or sleeper raised beds. Plants suitable for vertical planting will be found on pages 34–35.

This is a retaining wall rather than a raised bed, but it can support plants in the same manner.

11. Retaining Walls

Retaining walls are built to hold back soil, so that instead of having a sloping site, a series of flat levels or terraces can be made. In the example garden on page 5, terraces have been created above and below the rock garden, with a retaining wall above the lower paved area.

The walls can be built to any height that allows easy maintenance. It is important, however, to decide on a height that can be practically built, which usually means up to 5 ft (1.5 m). The wall shown here is about 3 ft (90 cm) high, which is not a difficult height for a householder to build, and is made of natural stone which is laid dry. Any mortared retaining wall should be done professionally as, according to the type of soil, each one requires drainage weep-holes to be installed at different levels.

Construction

Remove the top soil (the darker material) from the proposed building area, and place it to one side. Remove the sub-soil to a depth of 3 in (7.5 cm) along the line where the wall is to be built, and also take out 9 in (23 cm) of soil from the face of the bank that is to be retained, if you wish to plant the wall. The sub-soil can be disposed of or used to fill up behind the wall, if you are not going to plant the face.

Lay the first stones 3 in (7.5 cm) below ground level and leaning back at the rate of 2 in (5 cm) for every 1 ft (30 cm) rise of the wall, for stability. Try to avoid laying any stones with their vertical joints in line with one another, which would weaken the wall. Do not place any soil between the stones to fill the gaps, because this will only wash out later. (Have a look at the dry stone walls up and down the country which form the boundaries of many of our fields.) Where gaps do appear between stones either plant them, or fill behind joints with odd pieces of stone. To do this, the soil behind the wall will have to be filled in as the wall is built.

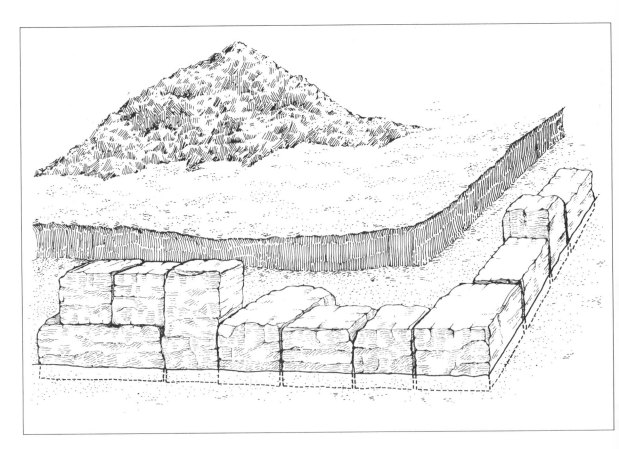

The bank has been cut away by at least 9 in (23 cm) beyond where the bottom stones lie. The stones have started to be laid 3 in (7.5 cm) below ground level. Now each corner will be built.

Soils

Any wall above 3 ft (90 cm) high, should have some longer stones inserted at regular intervals to run back into the bank and act as anchors. The soil surrounding them will hold the wall in place and prevent it bowing out under pressure from behind. As the wall builds up, fill in behind the wall with the soil mix recommended on page 14 for alpines and rock gardens, and the top soil that was put on one side immediately behind that, treading down each 6 in (15 cm) layer. Should there be a high wall, and a depth behind it of over 1½ ft (45 cm) to fill, use the sub-soil first, but at a distance from the wall of at least 15 in (38 cm). Always overfill by 1 in (2.5 cm) at least, to allow for the soil settling.

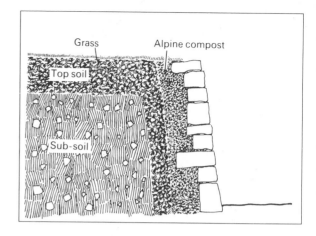

Grass and planting

As illustrated, the original site had a lawn on it. Save the best of this in strips 1 ft (30 cm) × 3 ft (90 cm) and re-lay it on the new site, starting nearest the wall. It can be laid either over the stones on the wall, or as far away as required to leave a bed for planting. If a space is left for planting, then the soil for 9 in (23 cm) depth must be of the soil mix for planting. The planting of the wall face should be carried out as the wall is built. Arrange for the stones to be shallow from the front to back where planting takes place, so that the roots will be in the soil, and the leaves and flowers on the wall face.

The completed retaining wall. Nails are inserted between the stones on each corner as it is built up, and strings stretched between the nails to give the line up.

12. Screes

The screes in nature are found on the sides of mountains which have had their exposed steep sides split open by a series of frosts, when ice expands their cracks, followed by thaws in the heat of the sun. The rocks break away and crash down the slope, breaking up further, until they form a pebble 'beach' on a steep slope, which gradually reduces in steepness. They are often associated with lakes at their foot, and have a great deal of water passing through them to the lake, and are continually on the move. The plants growing in them are naturally few and relatively small, and short-lived due to the movement.

Screes in gardens

A compromise is necessary in gardens, with no movement, good drainage, and soil under the pebble 'beach'. The need for water flowing through is not vital but a means of watering is, especially in the early stages.

Screes are the simplest form of construction to build, but the site needs to be right to be successful. The slope should not be more than 20 degrees and it can be much less. Even a slight fall in level will suffice, with the water table at least 1 ft (30 cm) below the lowest level of the site. The site can be surrounded by grass, but if it is, the grass must not contain any creeping grasses that can grow into the site, which will then be difficult to maintain. A neighbouring hard path, or rock garden or pond, or any combination of these near the site will also be successful, but not a shrub border, as this will have leaves which blow onto the site and be difficult to remove.

The site can be large or small, as long as it is in proportion to the size of the garden. If small it can appear as an extension of the rock garden.

The scree in late summer at the gardens of the Royal Horticultural Society, Wisley

Construction

If you use string to outline the site on the ground, it will make it easier to visualise what it will look like than if you use sticks and canes. Dig out the top soil and put it on one side. Then dig out the sub-soil, so that the total depth is about 1½–2 ft (45–60 cm). Dispose of the sub-soil as suggested on page 41. Use the removed top soil in the bottom of the scree bed, then add a compost of equal parts of loam, peat and grit on top, treading down each 6 in (15 cm) layer as you do so (see pages 14–15).

There is a choice of material for the top 4 in (10 cm), and the choice depends on the stone used. Match up the shingle, gravel or chippings according to the type of stone you want to site in the scree, as suggested on pages 12–13. It is on the scree that irregular or even rounded rocks can be used. The rounded ones will have to be used in isolation, because they do not join well. Several non-rounded ones may be laid to join together in a chain, or series of chains, with isolated ones dotted here and there. Too many will spoil the effect, but they are better if quite large. Lay them with the strata lines almost horizontal, taking care that all ends of chains and isolated rocks are partially buried at the back and sides as well. Avoid tall rocks but use spreading ones and some can be flush with the ground to serve as stepping stones for maintenance purposes, and save treading on plants or scree materials.

It is easiest to lay the rocks first on top of the soil then add the scree material afterwards. For appearance only, you could add broken material of the rocks used, to scatter on the surface, giving an impression of a scree in the wild, but this is not essential.

The whole effect will be of stones and rocks covered in patches of form and colour, none of which is very large. Suitable plants for the scree are dwarf conifers and shrubs (pages 36–37), cushion plants (pages 38–39) and dwarf bulbs (pages 48–49).

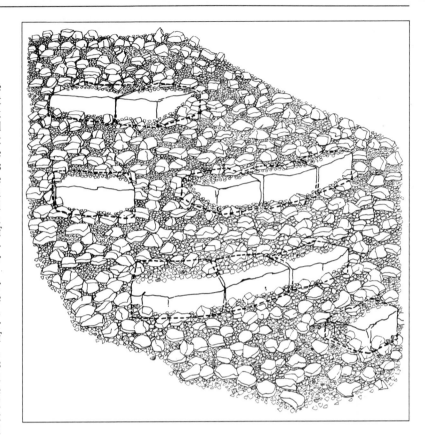

Typical scree bed on a gentle slope, with rocks set in a series of chains, and one isolated – ready for planting, and easy access to all parts without treading on the scree.

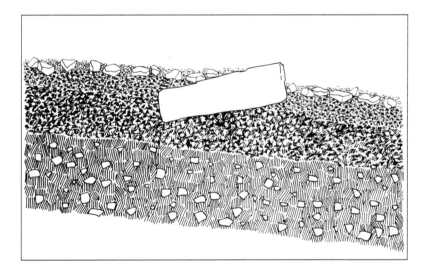

Cross-section of scree where rocks were laid before the surface material of shingle or similar. Shows how stable the rocks should be and how plant roots can reach cool areas under the rocks.

13. Plants for Vertical Planting

All the planting between stones and rocks must be carried out during construction, to give the plants the greatest chance of success. Choose good quality plants only – those which look fresh and strong. Avoid ones which have just been potted, and also old and woody plants with a lot of roots coming out of the pots. Whereas plants can be replaced easily enough on level ground, those planted between stones and rocks cannot, so choose carefully, and choose plants that will give colour over a long period.

The lists given below are a guide to the vast range of plants that is available, and are divided into three categories. The vigorous growers are intended only to cover large areas or eyesores, and are best not mixed with either of the other two categories. The medium and smaller-growing categories may overlap, depending on the soil and situation. Allow approximately 1½ ft (45 cm) spread down and across for each of the medium growers and 9–12 in (23–30 cm) each way for the smaller growers. The first measurement beside plants indicates height (out from the wall), and the second refers to spread.

E = evergreen; T = trailing or creeping; C = cushion; S = shrub; H = herbaceous.

Vigorous growers – All trail or creep unless otherwise stated.

Acaena 'Blue Haze' 4 in (10 cm) high, 6 ft (1.8 m) spread; bronze-grey foliage, reddish seed-heads in summer.
Ajuga reptans 'Rainbow' 6 in (15 cm) high, 4 ft (1.2 m) spread; multi-variegated foliage, deep blue flowers in summer, herbaceous.
Campanula poscharskyana 6 in (15 cm) high, 3 ft (90 cm) spread; mauve blue flowers in summer, herbaceous.
Cerastium alpinum lanatum T, 1 ft (30 cm) high, 4½ ft (1.35 m) spread; white flowers over grey foliage in summer.
Genista tinctoria 'Plena' S, 1 ft (30 cm) high, 3 ft (90 cm) broad; double, yellow flowers in summer, on slightly arching branches.
Oenothera acaulis 9 in (23 cm) high, 4 ft (1.2 m) spread; large foliage and flowers which are white to pink in summer, herbaceous.
Oenothera missouriensis Similar to above; large golden flowers in summer, herbaceous (illustrated opposite).

Phuopsis stylosa 9 in (23 cm) high, 3 ft (90 cm) spread; pink pin-cushions in summer, herbaceous.
Potentilla megalantha (syn. **P. fragiformis**) 9 in (23 cm) high, 1½ ft (45 cm) broad; golden yellow flowers all summer, herbaceous.
Vinca minor 'Bowles Variety' E, 8 in (20 cm) high, 3 ft (90 cm) spread; dark green foliage, mauve blue flowers in spring; for semi to full shade.
Vinca minor 'Variegata' E. Similar to above, but with cream and green variegated foliage.

The following trailing or creeping plants are also vigorous growers suitable for vertical planting and can be found on pages 46–47:
Alchemilla ellenbeckii, Arenaria balearica, Hedera helix 'Erecta', Hedera helix 'Sagittifolia', Helianthemum nummularium, Polygonum vaccinifolium, Prunella 'Blue Loveliness', Prunella 'Pink Loveliness', Prunella 'White Loveliness', Saxifraga Mossy hybrids, Trifolium repens.

Plants of medium vigour

Acaena microphylla T, 3 in (7.5 cm) high, 3 ft (90 cm) spread; tiny bronze red foliage, deep pink seed heads in summer.
Alyssum montanum 'Mountain Gold' T, S, 6 in (15 cm) high, 2 ft (60 cm) spread; golden yellow flowers in early summer over greyish foliage.
Alyssum saxatile 'Gold Ball' T, S, 1 ft (30 cm) high, 1½ ft (45 cm) broad; yellow flowers over greyish foliage in late spring.
Antennaria dioica T, E, 8 in (20 cm) high, 2 ft (60 cm) spread; paper-white flowers over grey foliage in summer.
Antennaria dioica 'Rosea' T, E, pink form of above.
Aubrieta hybrids T, 1 ft (30 cm) high, 2 ft (60 cm) spread; shades of red, pink, mauve flowers in early summer.
Campanula carpatica hybrids H, 1 ft (30 cm) high, 15 in (38 cm) broad; large, cupped, blue or white flowers in summer.
Campanula cochlearifolia and forms H, T, 6 in (15 cm) high, 15 in (38 cm) spread; blue or white thimble flowers in summer.
Campanula garganica H, T, 9 in (23 cm) high, 1½ ft (45 cm) spread; starry blue flowers with white centres in summer.
Campanula pulla H, T, 6 in (15 cm) high, 1½ ft (45 cm) spread; purple blue bell flowers in summer.
Ceratostigma plumbaginoides H, T, 9 in (23 cm) high, 2½ ft (80 cm) spread; blue flowers in late summer to autumn; good autumn leaf colour.
Dianthus deltoides and forms T, E, 1 ft (30 cm) high, 2 ft (60 cm) spread; mostly dark shades of red flowers in summer.
Dianthus 'Pike's Pink' T, E, 8 in (20 cm) high, 3 ft

(90 cm) spread; double pink flowers over blue grey foliage in summer.

Geranium dalmaticum   T, 4 in (10 cm) high, 2 ft (60 cm) spread; salmon pink flowers in summer.

Geranium subcaulescens   T, 4 in (10 cm) high, 2 ft (60 cm) spread; carmine mauve flowers with black centres in summer.

Lithodora (Lithospermum) diffusa 'Heavenly Blue' S, E, 8 in (20 cm) high, 4 ft (1.2 m) spread; blue flowers in summer; for acid soils only.

Ophiopogon planiscapus 'Nigrescens'   T, E, 9 in (23 cm) high, 2 ft (60 cm) spread; purple-black foliage, purple-black berries in late summer-winter.

Phlox 'Chattahoochee'   H, 1 ft (30 cm) high, 1½ ft (45 cm) broad; blue flowers with red eye, for shady places.

Phlox douglasii hybrids   H, 9 in (23 cm) high, 2 ft (60 cm) spread; pink, white, red, mauve, blue or violet flowers in early summer.

Phlox subulata hybrids   H, 9 in (23 cm) high, 2 ft (60 cm) spread; various colours as above in early summer.

Potentilla × tonguei   H, T, 6 in (15 cm) high, 1½ ft (45 cm) spread; orange flowers with red centres all summer.

Raoulia australis   T, E, 1 in (2.5 cm) high, 3 ft (90 cm) spread; silver mats with tiny pale yellow flowers in summer.

Sedum acre 'Aureum'   T, 3 in (8 cm) high, 2 ft (60 cm) spread; starry bright yellow flowers in summer. Can seed itself.

Sedum spathulifolium 'Cappa Blanca'   C, E, 3 in (8 cm) high, 1½ ft (45 cm) spread; yellow flowers in summer over grey foliage.

The following plants, described on other pages of the book, are similar in size to the above and are also

Sedum spathulifolium 'Cappa Blanca' (*left*) and *Oenothera missouriensis*

suitable for planting in a vertical position.

On pages 36–37: *Genista lydia, Iberis semperflorens, Leucanthemum hosmariense, Thymus citriodorus* 'Archer's Gold', *Veronica prostrata* (syn. *rupestris*), *Zauschneria californica*.

On pages 38–39: *Bolax* (syn. *Azorella*) *glebaria, Saxifraga × apiculata, Silene acaulis*.

On pages 44–45: *Anacyclus depressus, Mertensia asiatica*.

On pages 46–47: *Chiastophyllum oppositifolium, Dryas octopetala*.

Smaller growers

Androsace sarmentosa 'Chumbyi'   T, 4 in (10 cm) high, 2 ft (60 cm) spread; hanging rosettes of pink flowers in summer.

Androsace sempervivoides   T, 3 in (8 cm) high, 3 ft (90 cm) spread; pink flowers, darkening with age, in summer.

Antennaria dioica 'Minima'   T, E, 3–4 in (8–10 cm) high, 2 ft (60 cm) spread; grey foliage, with bobble heads of pink flowers in summer.

Campanula 'Birch Farm Hybrid'   H, 4 in (10 cm) high, 8 in (20 cm) broad; pale blue bells in summer.

Campanula sartori   H, 3 in (8 cm) high, 8 in (20 cm) broad; pale blue bells in summer.

Iberis 'Little Gem'   E, S, 6 in (15 cm) high, 1½ ft (45 cm) broad; white flowers in summer.

Lewisia cotyledon howellii   E, 6 in (15 cm) high, 9 in (23 cm) broad; large rosettes of fleshy leaves, apricot-pink flowers in summer. Only for growing vertically.

Phlox caespitosa   H, C, 6 in (15 cm) high, 1½ ft (45 cm) broad; white to lilac flowers in spring-early summer.

Potentilla cuneata (syn. **P. ambigua**)   S, T, 3 in (8 cm) high, 1 ft (30 cm) spread; yellow flowers in summer to autumn.

Saxifraga cochlearis 'Minor'   C, E, 8 in (20 cm) high, 1 ft (30 cm) spread; white flowers extending well beyond the tight rosettes of silver grey, in summer.

The following plants, described on other pages of the book, are similar in size to the above and are also suitable for planting in a vertical position.

On pages 38–39: *Armeria* 'Bevan's Variety', *Armeria caespitosa, Armeria maritima* 'Alba', *Asperula nitida puberula, Calceolaria* 'Walter Shrimpton', *Dianthus gratianopolitanus, Dianthus* 'La Bourbrille', *Dianthus* 'La Bourbrille Alba', *Dionysia aretioides, Draba aizoides, Saxifraga ×* 'Cranbourne', *Soldanella alpina*.

On pages 44–45: *Achillea argentea, Achillea ×* 'King Edward', *Artemisia schmidtiana* 'Nana', *Erinus alpinus* and *Erinus alpinus* 'Albus'.

On pages 46–47: *Asperula lilaciflora, Saxifraga oppositifolia* 'Ruth Draper', *Sempervivum* species.

14. Dwarf Conifers and Shrubs

Dwarf conifers are a confusing group of plants which, as the name implies, are smaller than their large brethren. Be careful when choosing any of them for a small site, or for a place where the rest of the plants would make a 6 ft (1.8 m) tall conifer look ridiculous. The list below only suggests plants growing up to 3 ft (90 cm) high or wide in up to 20 years, but there are many more which grow taller, yet are still termed 'dwarf'.

The shrubs vary considerably in their height and spread, but, unless otherwise stated, they will not grow above 2 ft (60 cm) high in fifteen years. Some may spread more than they grow vertically and these are termed 'spreading' in the text. Measurements given are approximate after ten years.

The conifers and dwarf shrubs form the backbone of any site, and should be planted first in all horizontal plantings. A few shrubs are suitable for vertical planting but only those described as such should be used in this position.

Dwarf Conifers – all evergreen

Abies balsamea 'Hudsonia' 1 ft (30 cm) high and broad; dark green broad needles.
Abies cephalonica 'Nana' 8 in (20 cm) high, 1 ft (30 cm) broad; prostrate habit, with dark green needles.
Abies concolor 'Compacta' 1½ ft (45 cm) high and broad; irregularly rounded habit, blue foliage, whitish in appearance underneath.
Abies procera 'Glauca Mabel' 1½ ft (45 cm) high, 15 in (38 cm) broad; a blue-grey Noble Fir.
Chamaecyparis lawsoniana 'Ellwood's Pillar' 15 in (38 cm) high; upright narrow growth, blue-green feathery foliage.
Chamaecyparis lawsoniana 'Minima Aurea' 1 ft (30 cm) high and broad; pyramid-shaped habit, yellow foliage.
Chamaecyparis lawsoniana 'Nidiformis' 10 in (25 cm) high, 20 in (50 cm) broad; dark grey-green foliage, flat-topped appearance.
Chamaecyparis obtusa 'Nana Lutea' 1 ft (30 cm) high, 8 in (20 cm) broad; bright golden foliage.
Chamaecyparis obtusa 'Nana Gracilis' 1 ft (30 cm) high, 10 in (25 cm) broad; shell-shaped, dark green sprays of foliage.
Chamaecyparis obtusa 'Pygmaea' 6 in (15 cm) high, 10 in (25 cm) spread; flattish appearance, bright green foliage.
Juniperus communis 'Compressa' 1½ ft (45 cm) high; columnar growth, blue-green small needles.
Juniperus horizontalis 'Banff' 6 in (15 cm) high, 1½ ft (45 cm) spread; feathery sprays of silver-blue foliage.
Picea abies 'Gregoryana' 10 in (25 cm) high, 15 in (38 cm) broad; dome-shaped growth, light green needles.
Picea abies 'Little Gem' 8 in (20 cm) high, and broad; bright green dome.
Picea abies 'Nidiformis' 8 in (20 cm) high, 10 in (25 cm) broad; darker than above and flatter topped.
Picea mariana 'Nana' 6 in (15 cm) high, 9 in (23 cm) broad; blue-green needles.
Picea pungens 'Globosa' 1 ft (30 cm) high and broad; rounded habit, spiky branches with silver-blue foliage.
Pinus mugo 'Humpy' 1 ft (30 cm) high and broad; dark green needles.

Dwarf shrubs – E = evergreen

Andromeda polifolia 'Compacta' E, 4–6 in (10–15 cm) high and broad; pink or white bells in summer.
Anthyllis hermanniae 2 ft (60 cm) high and broad; yellow pea flowers in spring.
Berberis × stenophylla 'Corallina Compacta' E, 2 ft (60 cm) high and broad; dark foliage, orange flowers in early summer.
Betula nana 1 ft (30 cm) high, 2 ft (60 cm) broad; dwarf birch.
Chamaespartium delphinensis 2 in (5 cm) high, 1½ ft (45 cm) spread; yellow flowers in summer, stems like green straps.
Daphne cneorum 'Eximea' E, 8 in (20 cm) high, 2 ft (60 cm) spread; scented, bright pink flowers in early summer.
Deutzia 'Nikko' 1½ ft (45 cm) high and broad; pale pink flowers in summer.
Euonymous fortunei 'Emerald 'n Gold' E, 1 ft (30 cm) high, and slightly broader; green and gold variegated foliage.
Euonymus minimus 'Variegatus' E, 6 in (15 cm) high, much wider spread; white and green variegated foliage.
Euryops acraeus E, 1 ft (30 cm) high and broad; yellow daisies in summer over silver-grey foliage.
Forsythia viridissima 'Bronxensis' 3 ft (90 cm) high and broad; yellow flowers in spring.
Genista lydia 1½ ft (45 cm) high, 2 ft (60 cm) spread; yellow flowers May to June.
Genista pilosa 'Procumbens' 6 in (15 cm) high, 2 ft (60 cm) spread; yellow flowers in summer.
Genista tinctoria 'Plena' up to 3 ft (1 m) high and broad; double yellow flowers in summer.
Hebe 'Carl Teschner' E, 8 in (20 cm) high, 1½ ft (45 cm) broad; blue-green foliage, violet flowers in summer.
Hebe 'Pagei' E, 6 in (15 cm) high, 1½ ft (45 cm)

Abies balsamea 'Hudsonia' (*above*), *Chamaecyparis lawsoniana* 'Minima Aurea' (*right*) and *Daphne cneorum* 'Eximia' (*below*).

broad; blue-green foliage, white flowers in summer.

Helichrysum tumida (syn. **H. selago var. tumidum**) E, 9 in (23 cm) high and broad; blue-grey corded foliage, white flowers in summer.

Hydrangea 'Pia' 15 in (38 cm) high and broad; domed pink flowers in summer; needs plenty of humus and moist conditions.

Iberis semperflorens E, 1½ ft (45 cm) high and broad; white flowers in winter to spring.

Leucanthemum hosmariense 1 ft (30 cm) high, 2 ft (60 cm) broad, with finely cut grey foliage, large white daisy flowers in spring.

Penstemon pinifolius 9 in (23 cm) high and broad; tubular scarlet flowers in summer, grassy leaves.

Polygonum vaccinifolium 6 in (15 cm) high, 3 ft (90 cm) spread; semi- or full shade, pink flowers in late summer.

Potentilla cuneata (syn. **P. ambigua**) 3 in (7.5 cm) high, 1 ft (30 cm) spread; golden yellow flowers in summer.

Potentilla fruticosa 'Elizabeth' 1 ft (30 cm) high, 2 ft (60 cm) spread; yellow flowers all summer.

Rhododendron impeditum E, 1½ ft (45 cm) high and broad; mauve flowers in spring to early summer and very small leaves; for acid soils only.

Thymus citriodorus 'Archers Gold' 8 in (20 cm) high, 1½ ft (45 cm) spread; golden, scented foliage.

Thymus citriodorus 'Doone Valley' 3 in (7.5 cm) high, 3 ft (90 cm) spread; dark green foliage flecked with gold, lavender pink flowers in summer.

Thymus serpyllum (syn. **T. drucei**) **'Albus'** 3 in (7.5 cm) high, 2 ft (60 cm) spread; white flowers in summer.

Thymus serpyllum (syn. **T. drucei**) **'Coccineus'** 3 in (7.5 cm) high, 3 ft (90 cm) spread; purplish-red flowers in summer.

Thymus serpyllum (syn. **T. drucei**) **'Minus'** 2 in (5 cm) high, 1½ ft (45 cm) spread; dwarf form of above with pink flowers.

Verbascum × 'Letitia' 9 in (23 cm) high and wide; grey foliage, spikes of yellow flowers in summer.

Veronica prostrata (syn. **rupestris**) 3 in (7.5 cm) high, 3 ft (90 cm) spread; deep blue flowers in early summer.

Zauschneria californica 2 ft (60 cm) high and wide; tubular scarlet flowers late summer to autumn.

Armeria maritima 'Alba'

Dianthus alpinus

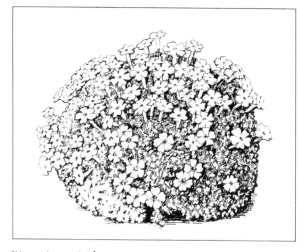

Dionysia aretioides

15. Cushion Plants

The term 'cushion' is used broadly to indicate those plants which grow in neat hummocks up to approximately 1 ft (30 cm) across, but not usually so high. They are easy to maintain once established because there is little or no pruning. They do require to be well drained, but need plenty of moisture during their growing period from spring to mid-summer.

You do not need to water the plants so often once they are established, and their roots are well down into the soil or under stones and rocks. For this reason watering, though vital during dry spells in the early stages of growth, becomes less essential for rock gardens, and retaining walls later on. For raised beds, however, watering may be necessary even when the plants are established, because the site is open all the way round.

Because of the relatively small size of cushion plants, it is advisable not to grow more vigorous plants too close to them. Creeping and trailing plants especially are the ones to beware of.

E = evergreen.

Armeria 'Bevan's Variety' E, 3 in (7.5 cm) high, 1 ft (30 cm) broad; pink flowers in spring to summer.
Armeria caespitosa E, larger than the form above.
Armeria juniperifolia 'Alba' E, 6 in (15 cm) high, 9 in (23 cm) broad; white flowers in spring to summer.
Armeria maritima 'Alba' E, 6 in (15 cm) high 1½ft (45 cm) broad; white flowers, spring to summer.
Asperula nitida puberula 2 in (5 cm) high, 6 in (15 cm) broad; neat white-tipped foliage, rose pink flowers in summer; herbaceous, but cushion habit in summer.
Bolax (syn. Azorella) glebaria E, 1 in (2.5 cm) high, 2 ft (60 cm) spread; hard, darkish green rosettes; for semi- or full shade.
Calceolaria falklandica 6 in (15 cm) high, 1 ft (30 cm) spread; large foliage on soil; dark yellow pouch flowers in spring to early summer on 4 in (10 cm) stems.
Calceolaria 'Walter Shrimpton' E, similar to above, but the pouched flowers more orange-yellow with maroon markings and a white lip.
Dianthus alpinus E, 4 in (10 cm) high, 8 in (20 cm) spread; pale to dark pink flowers in early summer.
Dianthus gratianopolitanus E, 8 in (20 cm) high, 1½ ft (45 cm) broad; light pink flowers in summer over blue-grey foliage.
Dianthus 'La Bourbrille' E, 4 in (10 cm) high, 9 in (23 cm) broad; pale pink flowers in summer over neat blue-grey foliage.
Dianthus 'La Bourbrille Alba' E, white form of above.
Dianthus 'Little Jock' E, 4 in (10 cm) high, 8 in

(20 cm) broad; pink semi-double flowers in summer over neat grey foliage.

Dianthus 'Mars' E, 4 in (10 cm) high, 8 in (20 cm) broad; clear red double flowers in summer over neat grey foliage.

Dionysia aretioides E, 2 in (5 cm) high, 6 in (15 cm) broad; light green foliage, bright yellow flowers in spring.

Draba aizoides E, 3 in 7.5 cm) high, 6 in (15 cm) broad; neat dark foliage, yellow flowers on thin stems in spring.

Draba bryoides imbricata 2 in (5 cm) high, 6 in (15 cm) broad; yellow flowers on thin stems in spring.

Gentiana acaulis E, 6 in (15 cm) high, 9 in (23 cm) broad; large, violet-blue trumpets, normally spring to early summer – can be later.

Gentiana verna E, 3 in (7.5 cm) high, 4 in (10 cm) broad; pale to dark blue flowers in spring.

Limonium minutum 4 in (10 cm) high, 8 in (20 cm) broad; pink everlasting flowers in summer.

Saxifraga × apiculata E, 4 in (10 cm) high, 1½ ft (45 cm) spread; yellow flowers in spring.

Saxifraga × apiculata 'Alba' E, white form of above.

Saxifraga × 'Bridget' E, 4 in (10 cm) high, 8 in (20 cm) broad; mauve flowers in spring over grey foliage.

Saxifraga × 'Cranbourne' E, 4 in (10 cm) high, 8 in (20 cm) broad; almost stemless flesh-pink flowers in spring.

Saxifraga 'Esther' E, 4 in (10 cm) high, 8 in (20 cm) broad; larger rosettes, soft yellow flowers in spring.

Saxifraga grisebachii E, 6 in (15 cm) high, 8 in (20 cm) broad; curious, mauve-red flowers on long stems in spring, silver foliage.

Saxifraga × jenkinsae E, 4 in (10 cm) high, 9 in (23 cm) broad; large, shell-pink flowers in spring, blue-grey foliage.

Saxifraga paniculata var. baldensis E, 6–9 in (15–23 cm) high, 10 in (25 cm) broad; tight silver rosettes, white flowers on arching stems in summer.

Saxifraga paniculata 'Whitehills' E, 6 in (15 cm) high, 8 in (20 cm) broad; red-edged, blue-grey rosettes, white flowers on arching stems in summer.

Silene acaulis E, 4 in (10 cm) high, 1½ ft (45 cm) spread; stemless pink flowers in summer over mossy green mounds.

Soldanella alpina E, 3 in (7.5 cm) high, 9 in (23 cm) broad; glossy, dark green foliage topped with frilly, dark mauve flowers in spring.

Soldanella pindicola E, similar but larger than above.

Teucrium chamaedrys 9 in (23 cm) high, 15 in (38 cm) broad; mauve-pink flowers in summer.

The following subjects (described on pages 34–35 under PLANTS FOR VERTICAL PLANTING) can all be included within this group of cushion plants: *Phlox caespitosa*, *Saxifraga cochlearis* 'Minor', *Sedum spathulifolium* 'Cappa Blanca'.

Gentiana acaulis

Saxifraga grisebachii

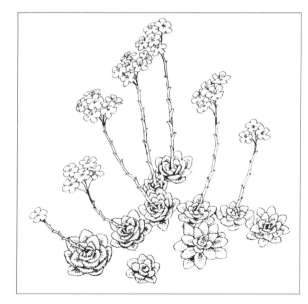

Saxifraga paniculata

16. Bog Gardens

Bog gardens are areas which vary from permanently moist to wet and muddy ground, which can be used for plants that do not actually need to be grown in water. Often there is a part of the garden that fits this description and appears to be a problem for the owner. This need not be the case, as there is plenty of plant material available to give a display of colour and form in the spring and summer and russet browns in the winter.

If such an area exists, it will be helpful to have good access across it without risk of becoming stuck in the mud. To this end, stepping-stones can be laid in close proximity though not necessarily touching. Use flat stones or alternatively tree chumps which have been cut in sections through tree trunks or large branches. Each stone or chump needs to be deep enough to be stable unless it is very wide or long. A 2 in (5 cm) thick slab must be at least 2 ft (60 cm) square in surface area, but thicker materials can have a smaller surface area. Plants can grow over parts of these slabs to take away any stark effect. The slabs are best laid flush with the ground.

Pool bog gardens

These features can be artificially installed in gardens that do not have any natural boggy areas. If a pool is to be built below the rock garden its size can be enlarged to incorporate a bog area within the pool, with an area of permanently moist ground immediately around it. Plants which require slightly different conditions can be chosen to grow in both these areas (see pages 42–43).

The diagram shows a liner pool in which a wall of concrete blocks, laid on the wide edge for stability but without mortar, has been erected. Place the first line of blocks on a fibreglass blanket to protect the liner, and place stones on top of the wall to hide it. The area within the liner will be permanently wet, whilst the area around the 'shoulder' will provide the moist conditions preferred by some plants.

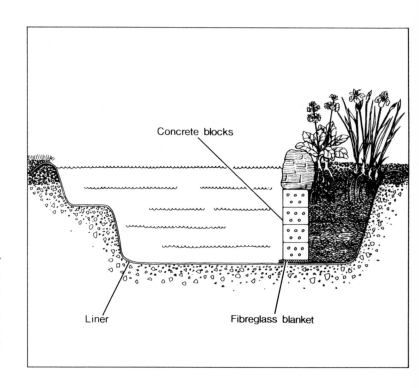

Concrete blocks

Liner

Fibreglass blanket

Artificial bog gardens without a pool

Where there is no pool, the ground can be contained so as to be moist, at least, in most parts of the British Isles and similar climates, and wet in regions where the rainfall is high enough. A level site must be used with a curved shape of simple design marked out where the area is wanted, and the top soil removed to one side.

Then remove the sub-soil to give a total depth of up to 2 ft (60 cm). It can be less in depth if the plants are only going to reach 2 ft (60 cm) in height. Then only 1½ ft (50 cm) need be removed. The sides of the hole should be steeply angled to prevent damage to the liner when planting. A liner of black polythene 250 gauge is laid in the hole with at least 6 in (15 cm) overlap around the edge to form a 'shoulder', which

should be buried as shown.

The 'shoulder' of the liner prevents the whole liner being pushed down further underground during maintenance operations. There must be at least 1 in (2.5 cm) of soil over the top of the 'shoulder' to prevent sunlight reaching the liner and breaking down the polythene with ultra-violet light, especially during the summer.

Punch a few holes in the base of the liner with a garden fork to prevent stagnation of water, then fill the base with well rotted manure, if this is available, up to 8 in (20 cm) in depth instead of replacing the sub-soil. If no manure is used, either garden compost, or top soil from areas to be paved will suffice. Then top this up with the top soil which was originally dug out from the hole. Each 6 in (15 cm) layer should be well trodden down to prevent the site sinking too much later on.

It is a good idea to mark the site in some way, so that a hoe or fork when used to disturb the soil surface does not interfere with the liner. If the site is not too wide, maintenance is easier and there will be no need to have slabs across the area. The sub-soil which was removed from the site can be disposed of in a hired skip, or by some other means, or used as a base soil for raised beds.

Water the site well after planting and keep it moist all the time by watering whenever necessary during the spring and summer. It should keep moist in the autumn and winter with the rain and the cooler temperatures.

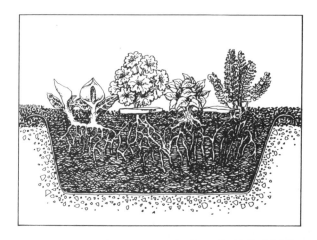

Two dazzling plants for the bog garden – *Mimulus* 'Whitecroft Scarlet' (*right*) and *Caltha palustris* 'Flore Pleno' (*below*). Both are described on the following pages.

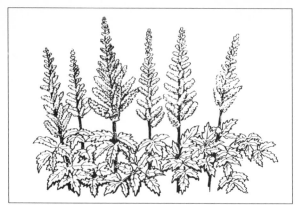

Astilbe chinensis 'Pumila'

Iris sibirica

Leucojum aestivum 'Gravetye'

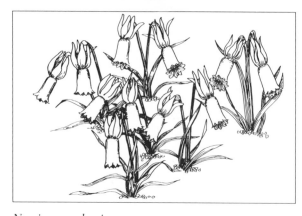

Narcissus cyclamineus

17. Bog Plants

These vary considerably in size, but the ones selected for this list are limited to a height of 3 ft (90 cm) and include many that are very much shorter. They can be grown in wet mud or just moist conditions and are given in two lists for the two different conditions. The plants for moist positions will tolerate very wet conditions for short periods only; similarly, plants for wet conditions will only endure dry ones for brief spells. Under no circumstances must the soil in either category ever dry out.

E = evergreen;   S = shrub;   H = herbaceous;
W = also suitable for wet conditions.

Plants for moist conditions

Anagallis tenella 'Studland' H, 2 in (5 cm) high, 3 ft (90 cm) spread; pink flowers in summer, acid soils only.

Andromeda polifolia 'Compacta' E, S, 4–6 in (10–15 cm) high and broad; pink or white bells in early summer. For acid soils.

Astilbe chinensis 'Pumila' H, 1 ft (30 cm) high, 9 in (23 cm) broad; divided foliage, pink flowers in summer.

Astilbe 'Fanal' H, 1½ ft (45 cm) high and broad; blood-red flowers in summer.

Cortusa matthioli H, 1 ft (30 cm) high and broad; short-lived plant producing plenty of seed, purple flowers in late spring to early summer.

Ferns H, or E, various sizes and shapes; for cool shade.

Hydrangea 'Pia' S, 1½ ft (45 cm) high and broad; ball-shaped pink flowers in summer.

Iris sibirica hybrids H, 3 ft (90 cm) high and broad; blue, white, mauve shades of flowers in summer. W.

Leucojum aestivum 'Gravetye' bulb, 2½ ft (75 cm) high, 1 ft (30 cm) broad; white flowers with green tips; the Snowflake flowers spring to summer. W.

Lobelia fulgens 'Queen Victoria' H, 2½ ft (75 cm) high, 1 ft (30 cm) broad; deep purple-red leaves and deep velvety scarlet flowers in summer.

Lysimachia nummularia 'Aurea' (Golden Creeping Jenny) H, 2 in (5 cm) high, 2 ft (60 cm) spread; golden-yellow foliage and flowers in summer; for sun or semi-shade. W.

Mimulus cupreus 'Minor' H, 3 in (7.5 cm) high, 15 in (38 cm) spread; large yellow-copper flowers in summer. W.

Mimulus primuloides H, 9 in (23 cm) high, 2 ft (60 cm) spread; smaller yellow flowers in summer. W.

Mimulus 'Whitecroft Scarlet' H, 3 in (7.5 cm) high, 15 in (38 cm) spread; large deep red flowers in summer. W. See illustration on page 41.

Mimulus 'Wisley Red' H, similar to above with large but paler red flowers. W.

Narcissus cyclamineus bulb, 9 in (23 cm) high; dwarf daffodil which spreads only slowly, golden yellow flowers with long tubes in spring.

Primula denticulata

Polygonum affine and forms 9 in (23 cm) high, 3 ft (90 cm) spread; pink to red flowers in summer.
Primula bulleyana H, 2 ft (60 cm) high, 1½ ft (45 cm) broad; orange flowers in summer.
Primula cockburniana H, 2 ft (60 cm) high, 1½ ft (45 cm) broad; orange-red flowers in summer.
Primula denticulata H, 1½ ft (45 cm) high and broad; mauve-blue or pink flowers in spring. W.
Primula denticulata 'Alba' H, white form of above. W.
Primula 'Garryarde Guinevere' H, 9 in (23 cm) high, 1½ ft (45 cm) broad; mauve-pink flowers in spring, over purple foliage.
Primula japonica H, 3 ft (90 cm) high and broad; tiers of deep pink flowers in summer.
Primula pulverulenta H, similar to above, but all parts of the plants have a white meal coating; red-purple flowers in summer.
Primula rosea 'Grandiflora' H, 6 in (15 cm) high, 1 ft (30 cm) broad; deep pink flowers in spring. W.
Primula vialii H, 2 ft (60 cm) high, 1 ft (30 cm) broad; mauve and red spikes of flowers in summer.
Saxifraga cuneifolia 'Variegata' H, 6 in (15 cm) high, 1½ ft (45 cm) spread; cream, pink, green foliage, pink flowers in summer; for semi-shade.
Saxifraga Mossy hybrids E, 6 in (15 cm) high, 2 ft (60 cm) spread; white, pink, red flowers in summer; for semi- to full shade.
Saxifraga fortunei E, 1½ ft (45 cm) high, 1 ft (30 cm) broad; bronze-green leaves which are sometimes purple beneath, topped by white flowers in autumn; for semi- to full shade.
Schizostylis coccinea and hybrids H, 1½ ft (45 cm) high, 1 ft (30 cm) broad; scarlet or pink flowers in autumn to winter. W.
Trollius acaulis H, 2 ft (60 cm) high, 1 ft (30 cm) broad; golden yellow flowers in spring to summer. W.
Trollius ledebourii H, similar to above, with orange flowers. W.
Trollius pumilus H, 1 ft (30 cm) high and broad; yellow flowers in spring to summer. W.
Zantedeschia aethiopica 'Crowborough' H, 2 ft (60 cm) high and broad; white arum flowers in summer. W.

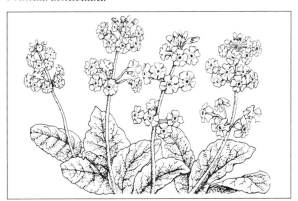
Primula japonica

Plants for wet conditions

Caltha palustris 'Flore Pleno' H, 1 ft (30 cm) high, 2 ft (60 cm) spread; double, deep yellow, flowers in spring. See illustration on page 41.
Cotula coronopifolia (Bachelor's Buttons) H, 4 in (10 cm) high, 3 ft (90 cm) spread over water surface; pale yellow flowers in summer.
Iris kaempferi 'Variegata' H, 2 ft (60 cm) high and broad; white and green variegated foliage, purple flowers in summer.
Iris pallida 'Variegata' H, 2½ ft (75 cm) high and broad; yellow and blue-green striped foliage, dark blue flowers in summer.
Menyanthes trifoliata (Bog Bean) H, 1 ft (30 cm) high, 10 ft (3 m) spread; pink buds opening into white flowers in late spring; can spread over water surface, but easily controlled.

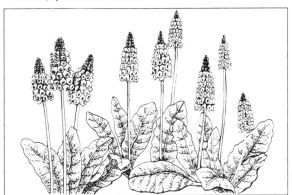
Primula vialii

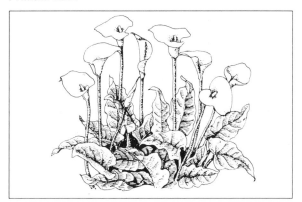
Zantedeschia aethiopica 'Crowborough'

18. Herbaceous Plants

These plants die down every winter, and the dead growths should be removed by early spring. Removal is usually easy if left until February, when the dead branches and twigs can be pulled out or broken away. The growth of most of these plants radiates out to form rounded or flat cushions and care must be taken to allow sufficient room for them to develop. If true cushion plants are nearby, then allow for the growth of both.

One advantage of herbaceous plants is that they can be lifted, divided and moved to new positions when the need arises. This is not true of other plants except creeping ones (see pages 46–47).

Achillea argentea   6 in (15 cm) high, 1½ ft (45 cm) spread; divided silver foliage, large white flowers in summer.

Achillea × 'King Edward'   6 in (15 cm) high, 1½ ft (45 cm) spread; divided silver foliage, buff-white flowers all summer.

Anacyclus depressus   3 in (7.5 cm) high, 1 ft (30 cm) spread; white daisy flowers with deep pink undersides in spring to summer.

Aquilegia akitensis   4 in (10 cm) high and broad; pale purple flowers in summer.

Aquilegia alpina   1 ft (30 cm) high, 6 in (15 cm) broad; deep blue or blue and white flowers, summer.

Aquilegia einseliana   9 in (23 cm) high, 6 in (15 cm) broad; large purple flowers in summer.

Aquilegia flabellata 'Nana Alba'   6 in (15 cm) high and broad; white flowers in summer.

Aquilegia formosa   1 ft (30 cm) high, 9 in (23 cm) broad; yellow or red and yellow flowers in summer.

Arnica montana   1 ft (30 cm) high and broad; large yellow daisy flowers in summer.

Artemisia schmidtiana 'Nana'   1 ft (30 cm) high, 1½ ft (45 cm) spread; mass of finely cut silver-grey foliage, white flowers in summer.

Campanula arvatica   6 in (15 cm) high, 9 in (23 cm) broad; blue, open bell flowers in summer.

Campanula carpatica 'Blue Chips'   6 in (15 cm) high, 1½ ft (45 cm) spread; large open blue bells in summer.

Campanula carpatica 'White Chips'   White form of above.

Campanula carpatica 'Wheatley Violet'   Violet form of above.

Campanula fragilis   8 in (20 cm) high, 15 in (38 cm) broad; purplish blue, white-centred flowers in summer.

Campanula 'Mist Maiden'   6 in (15 cm) high, 1 ft (30 cm) broad; white flowers in summer.

Campanula pulla   6 in (15 cm) high, 1½ ft (45 cm) spread; purple-blue bell flowers in summer.

Campanula warleyensis   4 in (10 cm) high, 15 in (38 cm) spread; pale blue double flowers in summer.

Erigeron compositus   6 in (15 cm) high, 9 in (23 cm) broad; white or pale mauve flowers in summer.

Erinus alpinus   3 in (7.5 cm) high, 6 in (15 cm) spread; pink flowers in spring to summer; can seed itself.

Erinus alpinus 'Albus'   White-flowered form of above with paler foliage.

Erinus alpinus 'Dr. Hanelle'   Darker pink form of *Erinus alpinus*.

Gentiana septemfida   6 in (15 cm) high, 1½ ft (45 cm) spread; purple-blue flowers in summer.

Gentiana sino-ornata   3 in (7.5 cm) high, 2 ft (60 cm) spread; if divided every three years, blue flowers in autumn; for acid soils only.

Hypericum olympicum   1 ft (30 cm) high and broad; large golden flowers in summer.

Iris setosa 'Dwarf Form'   4 in (10 cm) high and broad; purple flowers in spring to summer.

Mazus reptans   1 in (2.5 cm) high, 1½ ft (45 cm) spread; creeping plant, browny-green foliage, purple flowers with white and yellow markings in summer.

Mertensia asiatica   9 in (23 cm) high, 2 ft (60 cm) spread; large, blue-grey foliage, pale bluish-mauve flowers in summer.

Phyteuma scheuchzeri   15 in (38 cm) high and broad; deep blue, tubular flowers in summer.

Platycodon grandiflorum 'Apoyama'   15 in (38 cm) high, 1 ft (30 cm) broad; large balloon buds opening to blue flowers in summer.

Primula frondosa   6 in (15 cm) high and broad; white meal on grey foliage and flowers of mauve in spring.

Primula 'Tawny Port'   2 in (5 cm) high, 8 in (20 cm) spread; dark red foliage, blood red flowers in spring.

Pulsatilla vulgaris   15 in (38 cm) high, 1½ ft (45 cm) broad; deep mauve, or red or white flowers in spring, fluffy seed heads follow.

Campanula carpatica

Silene schafta   6 in (15 cm) high and broad; rose-magenta flowers in summer over grey foliage.

Viola cucullata 'Alba'   4 in (10 cm) high, 1 ft (30 cm) spread; white flowers tinged pale violet in summer; for semi-shade.

Viola 'Hazelmere'   6 in (15 cm) high, 9 in (23 cm) broad; mauve-pink flowers in summer; for semi-shade.

Viola stojanowii   3 in (7.5 cm) high, 8 in (20 cm) broad; rich yellow flowers in summer; for semi-shade.

Wahlenbergia albomarginata   9 in (23 cm) high and broad; white or blue open bell flowers in summer.

The following herbaceous plants are described on pages 34–35:

Campanula 'Birch Farm Hybrid', *Campanula cochlearifolia*, *Campanula garganica*, *Phlox* 'Chattahoochee', *Phuopsis stylosa*.

Pulsatilla vulgaris (*right*) and *Hypericum olympicum* (*below*) are beautiful additions to any rock garden.

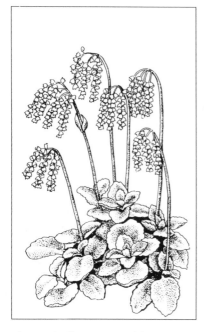

Arenaria balearica

19. Trailers and Creepers

Plants that trail have woody stems and are permanently above ground. They come from a single rootstock, but may root down into the ground as they grow. Creeping plants always put down roots as they grow, and some even do this over rocks and stones where apparently no soil exists. They collect dust particles, and soil is eventually made from this. This normally only occurs continuously in shady areas; it can occur in sunny ones during cool, moist and dull weather, but the plants' roots are burnt up by the sun when there is a period of drought, with a few exceptions.

Many plants in this list are suitable for vertical as well as horizontal planting and are referred to on pages 34–35; likewise, trailing plants described on those pages are mentioned at the end of this list. When plantings are made at the top of a wall to flow down, no vertical plantings should be carried out immediately underneath as the lower plantings will be smothered. E = evergreen.

Ajuga reptans and hybrids   6 in (15 cm) high, 4 ft (1.2 m) spread; different coloured foliages including wine, purple, variegated or dark green; blue flowers in summer.

Alchemilla ellenbeckii   6 in (15 cm) high, 3 ft (90 cm) broad; light green foliage, fluffy yellow flowers in summer, herbaceous.

Arabis ferdinandi-coburgii 'Variegata'   E, 4 in (10 cm) high, 1 ft (30 cm) spread; cream and green foliage, white flowers in spring.

Arenaria balearica   E, 2 in (5 cm) high, 6 ft (1.8 cm) spread; dark green mats, white flowers in spring to summer; acid soils in shade only.

Arenaria montana   4 in (10 cm) high, 1 ft (30 cm) spread; large white flowers in May to June.

Asperula lilaciflora 'Caespitosa'   2 in (5 cm) high, 1 ft (30 cm) spread; grey mats, soft pink flowers from spring onwards, herbaceous.

Asperula suberosa   2 in (5 cm) high, 1½ ft (45 cm) spread; grey woolly foliage, soft pink flowers, spring onwards, herbaceous.

Chiastophyllum oppositifolium   E, 6 in (15 cm) high, 1½ ft (45 cm) spread; yellow tassel flowers in summer.

Dryas octopetala   E, 6 in (15 cm) high 3 ft (90 cm) spread; creamy white flowers and fluffy seed heads in summer.

Hedera helix 'Erecta' (Ivy)   E, 9 in (23 cm) high, 3 ft (90 cm) spread; dark green foliage, semi- to full shade.

Hedera helix 'Sagittifolia' (Ivy)   E, 6 in (15 cm) high, 3 ft (90 cm) spread; white and green variegated foliage, semi- to full shade.

Helianthemum nummularium hybrids   E, 10 in (25 cm) high, 3 ft (90 cm) spread; red, yellow, pink, white flowers in summer.

Hutchinsia alpina   2 in (5 cm) high, 2 ft (60 cm) spread; white flowers in summer.

Sempervivum arachnoideum 'Laggeri'

Chiastophyllum oppositifolium

Mentha requienii 1 in (2.5 cm) high, 1 ft (30 cm) spread; scented foliage, herbaceous.
Polygonum vaccinifolium 6 in (15 cm) high, 6 ft (1.8 m) spread; pink heather flowers late summer to autumn.
Pratia pedunculata 2 in (5 cm) high, 3 ft (90 cm) spread; soft lavender flowers in summer.
Prunella 'Blue Loveliness' 10 in (25 cm) high, 1½ ft (45 cm) spread; blue spikes in summer.
Prunella 'Pink Loveliness' Pink form of above.
Prunella 'White Loveliness' White form of above.
Saxifraga Mossy hybrids E, 6 in (15 cm) high, 2 ft (60 cm) spread; white, pink, red, flowers in early summer, semi- to full shade.
Saxifraga × apiculata E, 3 in (7.5 cm) high, 1½ ft (45 cm) spread; yellow flowers in spring over bright green foliage.
Saxifraga × apiculata 'Alba' E, White form of above with paler foliage.
Saxifraga oppositifolia 'Ruth Draper' 2 in (5 cm) high, 1 ft (30 cm) spread; large, mauve-pink flowers in spring.
Sempervivum species and hybrids E, 6 in (15 cm) high, 1 ft (30 cm) spread; pink flowers in summer, rosettes of foliage small to large, green to red, some with white webs.
Silene acaulis E, 3 in (7.5 cm) high, 1½ ft (45 cm) spread; pink flowers in summer.
Thymus citriodorus 'Archers Gold' 8 in (20 cm) high, 1½ ft (45 cm) spread; golden, scented foliage.
Thymus citriodorus 'Doone Valley' 3 in (7.5 cm) high, 3 ft (90 cm) spread; dark green foliage flecked with gold, lavender pink flowers in summer.
Thymus serpyllum (syn. **drucei**) **'Albus'** 3 in (7.5 cm) high, 2 ft (60 cm) spread; white flowers in summer.
Thymus serpyllum (syn. **drucei**) **'Coccineus'** 3 in (7.5 cm) high, 3 ft (90 cm) spread; purplish-red flowers in summer.
Thymus serpyllum (syn. **drucei**) **'Minus'** 3 in (7.5 cm) high, 1½ ft (45 cm) spread; mauve-pink flowers in summer.
Trifolium repens 'Purpurescens' 4 in (10 cm) high, 4 ft (1.2 m) spread; purple-black and green variegated clover, herbaceous.
Veronica prostrata (syn. **rupestris**) 3 in (7.5 cm) high, 3 ft (90 cm) spread; deep blue flowers in early summer.

Trailing or creeping plants described on pages 34–35:
Acaena 'Blue Haze', *Acaena microphylla, Androsace sarmentosa, Androsace sempervivoides, Antennaria dioica, Antennaria dioica* 'Minima', *Antennaria dioica* 'Rosea', *Aubrieta* hybrids, *Cerastium alpinum lanatum, Geranium dalmaticum, Geranium subcaulescens, Lithodora (Lithospermum) diffusa* 'Heavenly Blue', *Ophiopogon planiscapus* 'Nigrescens', *Phlox douglasii* hybrids, *Phlox subulata* hybrids, *Sedum acre* 'Aureum', *Sedum spathulifolium* 'Cappa Blanca', *Vinca minor* 'Bowles Variety', *Vinca minor* 'Variegata'.

Dryas octopetala

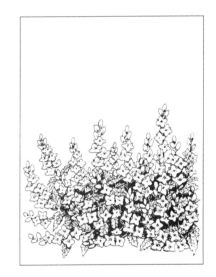
Veronica prostrata

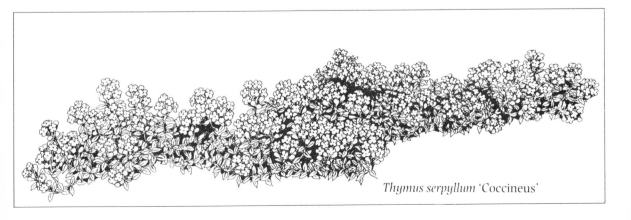
Thymus serpyllum 'Coccineus'

Allium beesianum

20. Dwarf Bulbs

Bulbs form some of the most colourful plants, and are the main plantings in alpine meadows. They grow just as well in many instances in rock gardens, raised beds, paving and on the top of dry stone walls. A few are suitable for sink gardens, as listed on page 55. The term 'bulb' is taken to include other storage organs as well, namely corms and tubers. Most of them die down shortly after flowering, except the autumn-flowering ones which die down in late spring.

All bulbs are for permanent planting and are not to be lifted and dried off in the dormant season. Always plant bulbs after all other plantings, otherwise they can be dug up by mistake. Do chart on paper where they are planted to avoid planting on apparently empty spaces.

Unless otherwise stated, the bulbs listed below are spring-flowering.

For meadows

Colchicums   All autumn-flowering with large spring foliage up to 2 ft (60 cm) high and broad; for sun or semi-shade.
Colchicum agrippinum   Lilac-purple flowers, chequered with white.
Colchicum autumnale   Large rose-pink flowers.
Colchicum autumnale 'Album'   Large white flowers.
Colchicum speciosum   Large pink to purple flowers.
Colchicum speciosum 'Album'   Large white flowers.
Crocus nudiflorus   6 in (15 cm) high; produces underground runners, rarely in same place in successive years; purple-blue flowers in autumn.
Crocus speciosus   8 in (20 cm) high; purple flowers in autumn.
Narcissus hybrids (Daffodils)   Most are large-flowered and naturalise well in grass. Up to 2 ft (60 cm) high.
Ornithogalum species (Star of Bethlehem)   6 in (15 cm) high. In most cases the flowers are shorter than the foliage. All have white or greenish-white flowers.

The white form of *Cyclamen hederifolium* (syn. *C. neapolitanum*).

For constructed areas

Allium beesianum   1 ft (30 cm) high; bright blue to purple-blue flowers in summer.
Allium cernuum   1½ ft (45 cm) high; rose-pink, purple or white nodding flowers in summer.
Allium cyaneum   9 in (23 cm) high; blue, bell-shaped flowers in summer.
Allium ostrowskianum   9 in (23 cm) high; grey-green foliage, rose-pink flowers in summer.
Iris unguicularis (I. stylosa) and hybrids   15 in (38 cm) high and broad; fragant lilac-blue, pink or mauve flowers in winter to spring.
Lewisia nevadensis   3 in (7.5 cm) high; white flowers shorter than foliage; dies down early; can seed itself.
Lilium formosanum 'Pricei'   9 in (23 cm) high; very large trumpet flowers of white with bars of red-purple on reverse in summer.
Rhodohypoxis baurii and hybrids   3 in (7.5 cm) high; red, pink or white flowers in summer; dies down in winter.
Sisyrinchium douglasii   9 in (23 cm) high; blue or white flowers in spring.
Sisyrinchium macounii 'Album'   9 in (23 cm) high; white flowers in summer.

For constructed areas and meadows

Anemone blanda and hybrids   3 in (7.5 cm) high, 1 ft (30 cm) spread; blue, red, pink or white flowers; for sun or semi-shade.
Anemone nemorosa and hybrids   6–9 in (15–23 cm) high, 1½ ft (45 cm) spread; white, pale blue, lavender or flesh pink flowers; for sun or semi-shade.
Crocus chrysanthus hybrids   8 in (20 cm) high; arching narrow leaves, various coloured flowers, including blue, yellow, white or cream, often with feathering on the outside.
Cyclamen coum   4 in (10 cm) high, 6 in (15 cm) broad; varying shades of pink to occasional white flowers in mid-winter to early spring, semi-shade.
Cyclamen hederifolium (C. neapolitanum)   8 in (20 cm) high, 15 in (38 cm) spread; pink or white flowers in late summer-autumn; for semi-shade.
Cyclamen repandum   4–6 in (10–15 cm) high, 6 in (15 cm) broad; slightly furled pink flowers, semi-shade.
Erythronium dens-canis (Dog-tooth Violet)   6 in (15 cm) high; rose-purple flowers with reflexed petals over brown-purple-marked, pale green foliage.
Galanthus species and hybrids (Snowdrop)   15 in (38 cm) high; white with green markings.
Galanthus nivalis reginae-olgae   12 in (30 cm) high; white autumn flowers appear without leaves.
Ipheion (syn. **Tritelia**) **uniflorum 'Wisley Blue'**   8 in (20 cm) high, spreads easily to 1 ft (30 cm) broad; mauve-blue flowers.
Narcissus bulbocodium and forms (Hooped Petticoat Daffodil)   8 in (20 cm) high; varying shades of yellow, open flowers; for semi-shade or sun, and acid soils.
Narcissus cyclamineus   9 in (23 cm); spreads only slowly; golden-yellow, long-tubed dwarf daffodil.
Narcissus pseudo-narcissus (Welsh Daffodil)   15 in (38 cm) high; golden yellow trumpet.
Narcissus triandrus 'Albus'   9 in (23 cm) high; cream flowers; dry, semi-shade is preferable.
Scilla siberica   6 in (15 cm) high; bright blue flowers; for sun or semi-shade.

The autumn-flowering *Colchicum speciosum* (*above*) belongs to a family of showy bulbs. The flowers of colchicums appear suddenly, bare of leaves. These do not come up until the spring when they make lush, rather coarse foliage until withering in the early summer. Colchicums are usually easy to grow and make a splendid addition to meadows. In other surroundings they need placing with care, as their leaves become large and can smother smaller plants.

Sisyrinchium macounii 'Album' is a good subject for constructed areas. It produces its relatively large, white flowers for a long period in summer above strap-like leaves which grow decoratively in fans. It is graceful and neat, although it can make quite a wide clump. Most sisyrinchiums are easy to cultivate and will self-sow, which may not be welcome in all surroundings.

21. Meadows

A grass area containing mainly bulbs is called a meadow, because the grass is only cut for a short period. Whilst the bulbs are growing and flowering, and for a short period afterwards when they are dying down, the grass is not cut at all. This period lasts from October to the end of June of the following year. The bulbs could be in flower for most of this period, given the range of different species available. Other plants can be grown in the meadow as well, but none must be shorter than 3 ft (90 cm) high otherwise they will be lost in the long grass of May and June, and may be accidentally cut down.

Types of grass

The grass does not need to be of good quality, but preferably should not contain running grasses. These can be harder to cut when the first cut is made. They will also spread to other parts of the garden with their runners more easily.

Choose shorter grasses if the meadow is started from scratch. A good mixture is 60% chewings fescue, 20% browntop bent and 20% creeping red fescue. This will save so much cutting, but where grass already exists use that rather than change it all.

Sow the grass seed first, then plant the bulbs, not the other way round; the bulbs may grow before the grass otherwise! Sow in the autumn of the first year, then plant the bulbs in the late summer to autumn of the second year. With established grass, plant the bulbs in the late summer and autumn.

Planting

Cut the grass quite close before planting to make the job easier. Divide the bulbs into groups of each sort for planting in irregular blocks. Do not mix them up together – for example, keep *Narcissus triandrus* 'Albus' in one group and *Narcissus bulbocodium* in another. Gently throw one group onto the area where they are to grow; this scattering will make their positions look natural. Then do the same for all the other groups before planting anything so that you can see where everything is going.

With a spade make a nick in the ground four times deeper than the bulbs. Push the spade back and forth until an opening is made wide enough to drop the bulbs in (it is easier to do this when the soil is moist). Fill the bottom of the trench with gritty or sandy soil so that the bulbs are not sitting on air, and so that the bulbs are about two and a half times their depth below ground (see the illustration of this).

Take the bulbs that are scattered nearest the spade for the first trench, and plant up to six bulbs (depending on their size) on top of the introduced soil. Make a further trench where there is another scattering of bulbs, but make sure this is not in line or parallel to the first

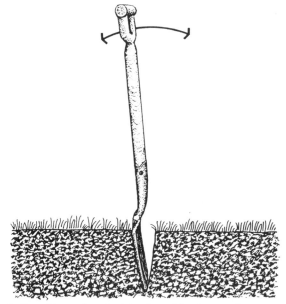

The spade is thrust in and rocked back and forth to make an opening wide enough to plant the bulbs.

The bulbs are planted about two and a half times their depth.

trench; and then follow this procedure for all the bulbs.

When all the planting is done,
go over all the trenches with your
feet and tread each of the trenches
inwards. This method of planting
saves a great deal of time and
effort, and the trenches will not be
seen after three weeks. Despite the
fact that the bulbs are being
planted in short rows, they will not
give this appearance when they
are growing.

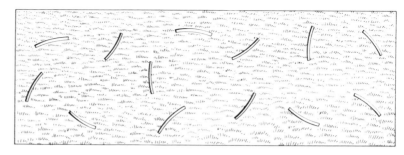

Spade thrusts in the meadow at varying angles to one another, each planted
with up to 6 bulbs depending on size.

Cutting the meadow

Flowering of the bulbs listed on pages 48–49 will
finish by early May, and the bulbs will have died down
naturally by late June. Cut the grass then. As it will be
long, there are two methods of cutting it. Very small
areas can by cut with a pair of shears, but larger ones
are more easily cut with a mowing machine which
can be hired for just one cut a year. A large rotary
machine is the best type. Rake off the grass that has
been cut and compost it. Then mow with another
machine and then, after that, mow the grass as
necessary. The time for cutting to stop is dependent on
when the first flowers or leaves appear for the next
year. Where autumn-flowering crocus and colchicums are grown, these are better confined to one
area of grass. This area is mown until late August.
Grass containing all other bulbs can be cut until late
September.

**The meadow is at its most decorative in spring when crowded with narcissus of all kinds. The small Hooped
Petticoat Daffodils (*Narcissus bulbocodium*) and *Narcissus triandrus* 'Albus' are particularly attractive, with
Erythronium dens-canis providing small splashes of rose-purple.**

22. Sink Gardens and Paved Areas

Sink gardens provide the opportunity for a really miniature form of gardening. They are easily adapted to any situation, and can be treated as enlarged pots for growing a variety of plants. The greatest range will of course grow in the sunnier situations, but shady positions offer possibilities as well.

Artificial stone sinks

The stone sinks which started the idea are now very rare and consequently expensive. Glazed sinks, however, are now being replaced by pressed steel units in our homes and these discarded sinks offer a very good alternative. They can be covered with a cement-based mixture, called 'hyper-tufa', which will look like real stone.

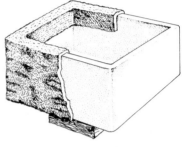

A glazed sink being covered with hyper-tufa. Put it on by hand, and wear household gloves to do so.

A glazed sink is best given a covering in the early autumn when it is cool, with less risk of frost, and there is more time for the covering to mature before the sink is planted in the spring. Use plastic sheets under the sink to save making an unnecessary mess. Household gloves should be worn to protect the hands and thrown away afterwards. If the sink is mounted in its permanent position when treated it will save handling it twice, and in any case always move it before filling it with soil. The mounting block or blocks need not be more than 9 in (23 cm) high and can be less.

1. Remove all pipe fittings from underneath, but the metal drain ring can be left in to reduce the size of the drainage hole. Thoroughly clean the sink and mount it on a block placed centrally beneath, ready for the hyper-tufa mix to go on.

2. Treat the outside, top edges, and at least 3 in (7.5 cm) down inside and 3 in (7.5 cm) underneath from the outside, with Unibond or similar adhesive, spread with a piece of wood. Allow this to dry for about two hours, then again coat part of the sink with the adhesive, spreading it over the top and inside, and underneath as before.

3. Allow the second coat of adhesive to become tacky, then begin applying the hyper-tufa. The mixture is in parts by bulk of $1\frac{1}{2}$ parts cement: 1 part builder's sand: 2 parts sieved peat. Mix together sufficient quantity to almost fill a plastic bucket, then add water until the consistency is that of toothpaste. The mixture is applied to small areas at a time, about $\frac{1}{2}$ in (1.5 cm) thick.

4. Before the first area is completed, apply adhesive to another, similar sized area, so that this can become tacky and ready for the application of the hyper-tufa. Repeat the process until the sink is covered. Should the adhesive dry too quickly, either treat smaller areas at a time or use more adhesive. Do not mix too much hyper-tufa at a time otherwise it will dry too quickly.

The glazed sink garden covered with hyper-tufa and mounted on its final block of stone or a similar support. The soil, stones and plants have been added.

5. Using a file, or a similar instrument, mark lines to simulate stone cuts in the mixture a few hours after completing the application. Then, twenty four hours after the mixture is applied, paint sour milk, or seaweed liquid feed (neat), over all the treated area with a paint brush. If this is done three times in quick succession, it will make the appearance much darker, especially when seaweed feed is used. The surface will soon settle down and age quickly with mosses and algae which make it look natural.

6. A piece of perforated zinc large enough to cover the drainage hole is all that is necessary for good drainage; or a larger sheet of fine mesh nylon can be used instead.

Placing the sinks

They can be mounted anywhere in the garden that has a hard surface, but they must be level for drainage purposes. If placed on paving, plants can also be planted in the paving at the base of the sinks to soften the site and make it more colourful. They should last from 5–15 years depending on their plantings.

Planting the sinks

The soil mix for the sink garden can be heavier than the type that is used for other structures. John Innes No 2 compost is ideal, with some additional grit for high rainfall areas, or additional peat for low ones. Firm the soil in well and fill until it almost reaches the sink top.

The stone for sink gardens does not follow the rules for other structures. Any stone can be used to add height or colour or form, or any combination. Avoid using small stones though, as these will be lost.

Tufa stone is creamy white when fresh but soon ages to grey, or a greenish or pinkish colour. Using a club hammer and cold chisel, holes can be chiselled in the tufa for planting, about 2–3 in (5–8 cm) deep, anywhere on its surface. These holes can be filled with a soil mixture of 1:1:1 (see pages 14–15). Use a potato peeler with a grooved channel down the middle as a trowel, and an old biro as a rammer. Only use young seedlings for planting, as those from pots will have too large a root ball. Place a little soil in the hole, ease the roots of the young seedlings into it, then add soil gently but firmly all round the roots until the head of the seedling rests on the outside of the hole. The roots will actually grow into the porous tufa.

Place any stones used onto or just under the soil surface and plant up to 15 plants in an average sized sink. Use small trailers near the edges to hang over the sides, and use a topping of chippings to match the stone used. Do this after planting to bring the soil level to just above the top of the sink.

Paving

Paving slabs come in a variety of shapes and sizes, and should be laid to have a slight slope (in order to run off rain) to one or more sides. Use a soil base where this is reasonably firm and avoid hardcore underneath where planting is to take place. The plants grow in narrow gaps in the paving but their insertion must take place during construction. The advantages of this method are that there is little or no weeding, the slabs join together tightly enough to prevent movement, and no soil washes out over the paving.

The other method is to leave out a few slabs at random for planting afterwards. It does allow for replacement planting. In all cases it is better if you can introduce the planting soil, in which case use a 1:1:1 mix (see pages 14–15).

The slabs are laid on firm soil, using a spirit level and long straight-edged boards. Up to 5 spots of mortar are placed under each one to a thickness of 2 in (5 cm) when laid, and then they are squashed out when the slab is tapped down with a wooden block. The mortar mix is in parts by bulk of 1 part cement to 3 parts builder's sand.

Euryops acraeus (*above*) and the lavender-flowered *Pratia pedunculata*(*right*) are suitable plants for paving. The lovely *Saxifraga* x *jenkinsae* (*below right*) is a subject for a sink garden, like the one shown below.

23. Plants for Sink Gardens and Paving

All sink garden plants will be small growers because of the limited size of their environment. The paved area plants can be larger, but will not include herbaceous plants; they can be too easily trodden on by mistake when pruned in the spring. There is some overlap in the choice of plants for both purposes, those for the sink garden being suitable for paving, but not necessarily the other way round.

The sink gardens must never be allowed to dry out, especially in the growing season from March to July, otherwise like plants grown in pots, they will grow hard and woody and may die.

The advantage of planting in paving is that the slabs retain moisture beneath them that the plants can use. Even so, avoid planting conifers in paving where it will be hot and dry, as they may scorch badly. Do not plant bulbs in small gaps in paving, because they will grow in formal lines. Instead plant them where they are wanted, in larger pockets with perhaps a deciduous shrub so that there are no bare patches of soil after the bulbs have died down.

Many of the plants given here have been detailed elsewhere in the book, and are given here in the form of a table for ease of reference.

E = evergreen, and all heights given include the flowers.

Plants for sink gardens

Name	Height	Width	Description
CONIFERS (All E)			
Abies balsamea 'Hudsonia'	1 ft (30 cm)	1 ft (30 cm)	Dark green, broad needles (illustrated on page 37).
Chamaecyparis obtusa 'Nana Gracilis'	2 ft (60 cm)	1 ft (30 cm)	Pyramid-shaped.
Juniperus communis 'Compressa'	1½ ft (45 cm)	6 in (15 cm)	Columnar, blue-green, small needles.
Picea abies 'Gregoryana'	10 in (25 cm)	15 in (38 cm)	Dome-shaped, light green needles.
Picea abies 'Little Gem'	8 in (20 cm)	8 in (20 cm)	Bright green dome.
Picea abies 'Nidiformis'	8 in (20 cm)	10 in (25 cm)	Darker green than above, flat-topped.
Picea mariana 'Nana'	6 in (15 cm)	9 in (23 cm)	Blue-green needles, dense globe.
DWARF SHRUBS			
Andromeda polifolia 'Compacta'	4–6 in (10–15 cm)	4–6 in (10–15 cm)	Pink or white bells in early summer. E.
Helichrysum tumida (syn. *H. selago* var. *tumidum*)	9 in (23 cm)	9 in (23 cm)	Blue-grey, corded foliage; white flowers in summer.
Verbascum × 'Letitia'	9 in (23 cm)	9 in (23 cm)	Grey foliage, yellow flowers in summer.
TRAILING PLANTS			
Androsace sarmentosa 'Chumbyi'	2 in (5 cm)	1 ft (30 cm)	Spreading mats of rosettes of clear pink in summer.
Asperula lilaciflora 'Caespitosa'	2 in (5 cm)	1 ft (30 cm)	Grey mats with soft pink flowers from spring onwards.
Asperula suberosa	3–4 in (7.5–10 cm)	1 ft (30 cm)	As above, with tubular pink flowers from spring onwards.
CREEPING PLANTS			
Androsace sempervivoides	3 in (7.5 cm)	3 ft (90 cm)	Rosettes with pink flowers, darkening with age in summer.
Antennaria dioica 'Minimus'	3–4 in (7.5–10 cm)	1 ft (30 cm)	Grey mats with bobble heads of pale pink flowers in summer. E.
Arabis ferdinandi-coburgii 'Variegata'	4 in (10 cm)	9 in (23 cm)	White flowers in summer on cream and green variegated foliage. E.
Saxifraga oppositifolia 'Alba'	2 in (5 cm)	1 ft (30 cm)	White flowers in spring. E.
Saxifraga oppositifolia 'Ruth Draper'	2 in (5 cm)	1 ft (30 cm)	Darker foliage than above; large, deep mauve-pink flowers in spring. E.
CUSHION PLANTS			
Armeria 'Bevan's Variety'	4 in (10 cm)	1 ft (30 cm)	Pink flowers, spring to summer. E.

Armeria caespitosa	4 in (10 cm)	1 ft (30 cm)	Similar to above. E.
Asperula nitida	1 in (2.5 cm)	9 in (23 cm)	Rose-pink flowers in summer.
Calceolaria falkandica	6 in (15 cm)	1 ft (30 cm)	Large foliage on soil; dark yellow, pouch flowers in spring to early summer on 4 in (10 cm) stems. E.
Calceolaria 'Walter Shrimpton'	6 in (15 cm)	1 ft (30 cm)	Similar to above, but more orange-yellow flowers, with a white lip and maroon markings. E.
Dianthus alpinus	4 in (10 cm)	8 in (20 cm)	Pale to dark pink flowers in early summer (illustrated on page 38).
Dianthus 'La Bourbrille'	4 in (10 cm)	9 in (23 cm)	Pale pink flowers over neat grey foliage in summer. E.
Dianthus 'La Bourbrille Alba'	4 in (10 cm)	9 in (23 cm)	White form of above. E.
Dianthus 'Little Jock'	4 in (10 cm)	8 in (20 cm)	Pink, semi-double flowers over grey foliage in summer. E.
Dianthus 'Mars'	4 in (10 cm)	8 in (20 cm)	Double, clear red flowers over grey foliage. E.
Dionysia aretioides	2 in (5 cm)	9 in (23 cm)	Light green foliage, bright yellow flowers in spring (illustrated on page 38). E.
Draba aizoides	3 in (7.5 cm)	6 in (15 cm)	Dark, neat foliage with yellow flowers on thin stems in spring. E.
Draba bryoides imbricata	2 in (5 cm)	6 in (15 cm)	Yellow flowers on thin stems in spring.
Gentiana acaulis	6 in (15 cm)	9 in (23 cm)	Violet-blue, large trumpets, normally spring to summer – can be later (illustrated on page 39). E.
Gentiana verna	3 in (7.5 cm)	4 in (10 cm)	Pale to dark blue flowers in spring. E.
Lewisia cotyledon howellii	6 in (15 cm)	9 in (23 cm)	Plant only vertically between stones. Large rosettes of fleshy leaves, apricot-pink flowers in early summer. E.
Limonium minutum	4 in (10 cm)	8 in (20 cm)	Pink flowers in summer.
Saxifraga 'Bridget'	4 in (10 cm)	8 in (20 cm)	Broad, mauve flowers in spring over grey foliage. E.
Saxifraga × 'Cranbourne'	4 in (10 cm)	9 in (23 cm)	Flesh-pink flowers in spring. E.
Saxifraga 'Esther'	4 in (10 cm)	8 in (20 cm)	Larger rosettes with soft yellow flowers in spring. E.
Saxifraga grisebachii	6 in (15 cm)	8 in (20 cm)	Curious, mauve-red flowers on long stems in spring, silver foliage. E.
Saxifraga × *jenkinsae*	4 in (10 cm)	9 in (23 cm)	Large, shell-pink flowers in spring, blue-grey foliage (illustrated on page 53). E.
Saxifraga oppositifolia 'Alba'	See above (CREEPING PLANTS)		
Saxifraga oppositifolia 'Ruth Draper'	See above (CREEPING PLANTS)		
Saxifraga paniculata var. *baldensis*	6–9 in (15–23 cm)	10 in (25 cm)	Arching sprays of white flowers in summer on tight silver mats. E.
Saxifraga 'Whitehills'	6 in (15 cm)	9 in (23 cm)	Long spikes of white flowers on arching stems in summer over blue-grey foliage, edged red. E.
Sempervivum hybrids and species	up to 6 in (15 cm)	1 ft (30 cm)	Rosettes of foliage, small to large, green to red, some with white webs; pink flowers in summer (see illustration on page 46). E.
Soldanella alpina	4 in (10 cm)	8 in (20 cm)	Round, dark, glossy green leaves, frilly dark mauve flowers in spring. E.

BULBS

Cyclamen coum	4 in (10 cm)	6 in (15 cm)	Varying shades of pink to occasional white flowers in mid-winter to early spring.
Cyclamen repandum	6 in (15 cm)	6 in (15 cm)	Slightly furled, pink flowers in late spring.
Narcissus bulbocodium	4 in (10 cm)		Pale to dark yellow 'Hooped Petticoats' in spring.
Narcissus cyclamineus	6 in (15(cm)		Long, dark yellow trumpets in early spring (illustrated on page 42).
Narcissus triandrus 'Albus'	6 in (15 cm)		'Angel's Tears' – cream flowers in late spring.

Plants for paving

Name	Height	Width	Description
CONIFERS (All E)			
Abies cephalonica 'Nana'	8 in (20 cm)	1 ft (30 cm)	Prostrate habit with dark green needles.
Abies concolor 'Compacta'	1½ ft (45 cm)	15 in (38 cm)	Irregularly rounded habit, whitish in appearance underneath.
Abies procera 'Glauca Mabel'	6 in (15 cm)	1 ft (30 cm)	Blue-grey Noble Fir.
Chamaecyparis lawsoniana 'Ellwood's Pillar'	15 in (38 cm)	8 in (20 cm)	Upright narrow growth and blue-green foliage.
Chamaecyparis lawsoniana 'Minima Aurea'	1 ft (30 cm)	1 ft (30 cm)	Soft golden foliage (illustrated on page 37).
Chamaecyparis lawsoniana 'Nidiformis'	10 in (25 cm)	1½ ft (45 cm)	Grey-green branches.
Chamaecyparis obtusa 'Nana Aurea'	1 ft (30 cm)	10 in (25 cm)	Shell-shaped sprays of golden foliage.
Chamaecyparis obtusa 'Pygmaea'	6–8 in (15–20 cm)	up to 2 ft (60 cm)	Fan-shaped branches, leaves bronze in winter.
Juniperus horizontalis 'Banff'	6 in (15 cm)	1½ ft (45 cm)	Forms carpets; silver-blue foliage.
Picea pungens 'Globosa'	1½ ft (45 cm)	1½ ft (45 cm)	Spiky habit with silver-blue needles.
Pinus mugo 'Humpy'	1 ft (30 cm)	1 ft (30 cm)	Dense and bushy; dark green needles.
Pinus strobus 'Prostrata'	8 in (20 cm)	2 ft (60 cm)	Blue-grey foliage in a low mound.
DWARF SHRUBS			
Anthyllis hermanniae	2 ft (60 cm)	2 ft (60 cm)	Yellow flowers in spring.
Berberis × stenophylla 'Corallina Compacta'	2 ft (60 cm)	2 ft (60 cm)	Dark foliage, orange flowers in summer. E.
Chamaespartium delphinensis	2 in (5 cm)	1½ ft (45 cm)	Yellow flowers in summer.
Daphne cneorum 'Eximea'	8 in (20 cm)	2 ft (60 cm)	Scented, bright pink flowers in early summer. E.
Euonymus 'Emerald 'n Gold'	1 ft (30 cm)	1½ ft (45 cm)	Green and gold variegated foliage. E.
Euonymus minimus 'Variegatus'	6 in (15 cm)	1½ ft (45 cm)	White and green variegated foliage. E.
Euryops acraeus	1 ft (30 cm)	1 ft (30 cm)	Yellow daisies in summer over silver foliage (illustrated on page 53). E.
Genista lydia	1½ ft (45 cm)	2 ft (60 cm)	Arching stems and yellow flowers May to June.
Genista pilosa 'Procumbens'	6 in (15 cm)	2 ft (60 cm)	Yellow flowers in summer.
Genista tinctoria 'Plena'	up to 3 ft (90 cm)	up to 3 ft (90 cm)	Double yellow flowers in summer.
Hebe 'Carl Teschner'	8 in (20 cm)	1½ ft (45 cm)	Violet flowers in summer. E.
Hebe 'Pagei'	6 in (15 cm)	1½ ft (45 cm)	Blue-green foliage, white flowers in summer. E.
Iberis semperflorens	1½ ft (45 cm)	1½ ft (45 cm)	White flowers in winter to spring. E.
Leucanthemum hosmariense	1 ft (30 cm)	2 ft (60 cm)	Finely cut grey foliage, large white daisies in spring.
Penstemon pinifolius	9 in (23 cm)	9 in (23 cm)	Grassy leaves and scarlet, tubular flowers in summer.
Polygonum vaccinifolium	6 in (15 cm)	3 ft (90 cm)	Semi- or full shade; spikes of pink flowers in late summer.
Potentilla fruticosa 'Elizabeth'	1 ft (30 cm)	2 ft (60 cm)	Yellow flowers all summer.
TRAILING AND CREEPING PLANTS			
Acaena 'Blue Haze'	4 in (10 cm)	6 ft (1.8 m)	Bronze-grey foliage, reddish seed-heads in summer.
Acaena microphylla	3 in (7.5 cm)	3 ft (90 cm)	Bronze-red foliage, deep pink seed-heads in summer.
Antennaria dioica	8 in (20 cm)	2 ft (60 cm)	Paper-white flowers over grey foliage in summer. E.
Antennaria dioica 'Rosea'	8 in (20 cm)	2 ft (60 cm)	Pink form of above.
Aubrieta hybrids	8 in (20 cm)	2 ft (60 cm)	Shades of pink, red, mauve flowers in spring to early summer.
Cerastium alpinum lanatum	1 ft (30 cm)	4½ ft (1.35 m)	White flowers in summer over grey foliage.
Chiastophyllum oppositifolium	8 in (20 cm)	1½ ft (45 cm)	Yellow tassel flowers in summer (illustrated on page 46). E.

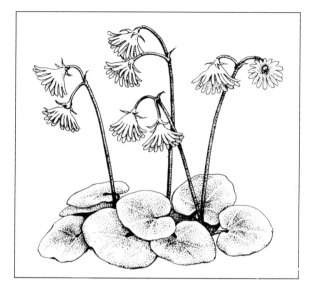

Antennaria dioica 'Rosea'   *Soldanella alpina*

Dryas octopetala	6 in (15 cm)	3 ft (90 cm)	Creamy white flowers and fluffy seed-heads in summer (illustrated on page 47). E.
Hedera helix 'Erecta' (Ivy)	1 ft (30 cm)	3 ft (90 cm)	Dark green foliage, semi- to full shade. E.
Hedera helix 'Sagittifolia' (Ivy)	8 in (20 cm)	3 ft (90 cm)	White and green variegated foliage, semi- to full shade. E.
Helianthemum nummularium hybrids	8 in (20 cm)	3 ft (90 cm)	Red, yellow, pink or white flowers in summer.
Hutchinsia alpina	2 in (5 cm)	2 ft (60 cm)	White flowers in summer.
Lithodora (Lithospermum) diffusa 'Heavenly Blue'	8 in (20 cm)	4 ft (1.2 m)	Blue flowers in summer; acid soils only. E.
Mentha requienii	1 in (2.5 cm)	1 ft (30 cm)	Scented foliage, herbaceous.
Phlox douglasii hybrids	6 in (15 cm)	2 ft (60 cm)	Various colours in early summer.
Phlox subulata hybrids	6 in (15 cm)	2 ft (60 cm)	Various colours in early summer.
Pratia pedunculata	2 in (5 cm)	3 ft (90 cm)	Soft lavender flowers in summer (illustrated on page 53).
Saxifraga Mossy hybrids	6 in (15 cm)	2 ft (60 cm)	White, pink, red flowers in early summer; semi- to full shade. E.
Sedum acre 'Aureum'	3 in (7.5 cm)	2 ft (60 cm)	Bright yellow flowers in summer.
Sedum spathulifolium 'Cappa Blanca'	3 in (7.5 cm)	1½ ft (45 cm)	Yellow flowers over grey foliage in summer. E.
Thymus citriodorus 'Archer's Gold'	8 in (20 cm)	1½ ft (45 cm)	Golden, scented foliage.
Thymus citriodorus 'Doone Valley'	3 in (7.5 cm)	3 ft (90 cm)	Dark green foliage flecked with gold; lavender-pink flowers in summer.
Thymus serpyllum (syn. *drucei*) 'Albus'	3 in (7.5 cm)	2 ft (60 cm)	White flowers in summer.
Thymus serpyllum (syn. *drucei*) 'Coccineus'	3 in (7.5 cm)	3 ft (90 cm)	Mauve flowers in summer (illustrated on page 47).
Thymus serpyllum (syn. *drucei*) 'Minus'	3 in (7.5 cm)	1½ ft (45 cm)	Mauve-pink flowers in summer.
Veronica prostrata (syn. *rupestris*)	3 in (7.5 cm)	3 ft (90 cm)	Deep blue flowers in early summer (illustrated on page 47).

CUSHION PLANTS

Armeria juniperifolia 'Alba'	6 in (15 cm)	1 ft (30 cm)	White flowers in spring. E.
Armeria maritima	9 in (15 cm)	1½ ft (45 cm)	Pink flowers in spring. E.
Bolax glebaria	2 in (5 cm)	1½ ft (45 cm)	Tight rosette foliage for moist semi- or full shade. E.
Silene acaulis	4 in (10 cm)	1½ ft (45 cm)	Pink flowers in summer. E.
Soldanella pindicola	4 in (10 cm)	1 ft (30 cm)	Frilly mauve flowers in spring.
Teucrium chamaedrys	9 in (23 cm)	15 in (38 cm)	Mauve-pink flowers in summer.

24. Monthly Work Schedule

JANUARY

– If ice forms on any pond to a depth of 4 in (10 cm) or more, use a container like a washing-up liquid bottle filled with hot water to pierce a hole in the ice. This enables the toxic gases which form under the ice to escape. The fish will not suffer from pressure of ice, but they will suffer if the ice is broken by hammer blows. Release the gases once a week for as long as the ice is still forming and this will help to maintain healthy fish.
– Construction work can be started or continued but it would be better to finish this by March at the latest to enable other routine work to be carried out.

FEBRUARY

– Remove all dead material from the herbaceous plants by pulling away dead leaves, and snapping off as low as possible all old, twiggy flowering stems.

MARCH

An upright herbaceous plant, showing spring buds at the base, is cut just above the buds.

– Continue as for February.
– The leafmould or compost which has been saved can be used on the shrub and herbaceous borders, as a mulch to conserve moisture and smother weeds.
– Order and buy plants for immediate planting (see April as well). Start the weeding programme by removing all weeds that have grown during the winter. Use a hand fork on all raised structures to disturb exposed soil to a depth of at least 1 in (2.5 cm).
– Use a simazine-based weedkiller on all paths and paved areas which are not planted. The effect should last for the season provided that there is no rain for twenty-four hours after application. It must be done during calm weather to prevent drift onto garden plants.
– Re-insert the waterfall pump in the base pool and use it regularly to keep it in good working order whilst it is under water.
– Every third to fifth year, lift and divide most bog plants. Dig in manure or compost which has been well rotted, inserting it at least 6 in (15 cm) underground. Divide and replant (see pages 60–61 for division techniques).

APRIL

– Remove any dead bulb foliage by pulling it away when it has completely died down. Do not tie the narcissus foliage in knots as this will affect regeneration of the bulbs for flowering the following year. Remove old flower heads of narcissus as they wither, to encourage regeneration.
– Planting can be continued, particularly during wet weather to save watering. Water newly planted areas, if the ground is dry, after planting.
– Top dress the raised areas if these have sunk at all. Only top dress with up to ½ in (1.5 cm) of whatever material tops the surface, at a time. Too much will bury the plants and kill them. Feed the plants in every raised structure every second or third year as recommended on page 15.
– Take glass covers off all plants when the weather is dry and store the glass and wires, after cleaning, wrapped in paper to keep them ready for next winter's use.
– Look for aphids on young growths and use a proprietary brand of systemic insecticide for aphids. Where algae are developing as surface scum on the ponds, scoop it off as soon as it appears with a bamboo rake or similar tool. Do not change the water, as this only makes it worse.

MAY

– Continue as for April: namely, check weeding; take leaves off dormant bulbs; complete any late planting; attend to watering, especially in the case of new plantings; scoop algae off ponds; check for aphids. Also check for lily beetle on lilies and fritillarias. These are bright scarlet and about ½ in (1.5 cm) long. Treat with a proprietary brand of contact pesticide, as systemics will not work.

– Cut back all flowering growths on aubrieta, after flowering is finished, with a pair of shears.

JUNE, JULY, AUGUST

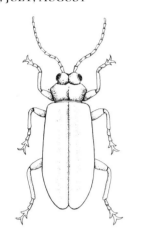

Waterlily beetle

– Check as for May. Also check for waterlily beetle, which shows on waterlily leaves as round chew marks or holes. To treat this, place two layers of newspaper on top of all the leaves (the paper must cover them entirely). Water will soak into the newspaper and push the leaves under the pond water and drown the beetle larvae. The papers can be put on in the evening and removed in the early morning. Do this once a week throughout the summer. About once a month, remove all waterlily leaves which have died, taking them right back to the crown of the plant, and compost them.
– When helianthemums and alpine phlox have finished flowering, cut back all flowering growths with a pair of shears.
– Collect seeds to swap with friends or to sow.
– Propagate by cuttings and sow seed as required (see page 60–61).
– In late June cut the meadow for the first time and continue each week as necessary (see pages 50–51). Feed the meadow with bonemeal at the rate of 2 oz per sq yd (70 g per sq m) every 3 years in August. Use a 2–4–D hormone killer on the meadow every three years to check broadleaf weeds. But this must not be applied within 3 ft (90 cm) of any water areas, nor should it be applied during very dry weather.
– Start planting bulbs.

SEPTEMBER

– Stop cutting that part of the meadow where the autumn-flowering bulbs are grown at the end of August. Stop mowing the remainder at the end of this month.
– Check watering, weeding, aphid control and continue taking algae off the ponds.
– Plant most of the bulbs needed for the meadow and all structures that have been built.

OCTOBER

A glass cover to protect the plant underneath from winter wet

– Netting used to protect fruit can be laid over any ponds before the leaves start to fall off the trees and shrubs. Peg it down with wires to catch the leaves as they fall, and empty the net weekly, otherwise they will accumulate and exclude light from the ponds.
– Sheets of glass can be placed over plants which are subject to botrytis grey mould damage due to wet and cold weather. Plants which have grey or blue foliage, small cushion plants or those with hairy foliage should be covered by the glass, large enough to extend over the plant with a little extra allowed as well. They are suspended over the plants on wires bent as illustrated. Plenty of light and air is admitted but no rain.
– Take leaves off the alpine and rock plant areas each week. Do not cut down herbaceous plants until the spring.
– Remove the water-circulating pump when the leaves start falling, disconnecting it only when the mains supply is switched off. Have the pump serviced by a reputable company, then store it for the winter in a dry shed or garage.
– Construction work of all types can be started this month now that the weather is cooler, and with no mowing, weeding or watering to be done.

NOVEMBER, DECEMBER

– Construction work can be started or continued.
– Remove leaves everywhere including off the netting over the ponds. It is particularly important to get leaves off the meadow by December to prevent them smothering the grass and bulbs. Remove the netting from the ponds by late December, or once the leaves have finally stopped falling, and have been removed from the whole garden. Compost all the leaves, to use as leafmould, or mix with other compost. This can be used on the borders as a mulch when rotted down for a year.
– Sow seeds of all alpines and rock plants that were late in setting seed (see pages 60–61).

25. Propagation of Alpines

Probably the most exciting of all operations is to reproduce plants for your garden. Facilities do not have to be elaborate, but attention to detail is important.

Garden frame

A simple frame of four wooden sides placed over a piece of ground in the shade, away from possible flooding, is all that is necessary to contain the pots of seeds and cuttings. Only a slight fall is required to run water off a glass or rigid plastic light, but a steeper slope is necessary for a polythene one to prevent the polythene sagging when wet. There is no need to make fancy joints in the walls of the frame; butt joints are fine.

The glass, or polythene, cover is less simple, but if the frame of this cover is not made with proper mitre joints, it can be constructed quite simply with flat L-brackets, as shown in the diagram. Check that the diagonal measurements are equal to ensure that the corners are square. The glass can be fixed to the cover frame by sticking insulation tape around its edges and holding it in place with electric cable clips. When polythene of 150 gauge is used, stretch a sheet over the cover frame and fix it with thin wooden battens; change the sheet every autumn as old material will split easily during bad weather in the winter.

When the frame is complete, cover the ground inside it with horticultural sand, and it is ready for use.

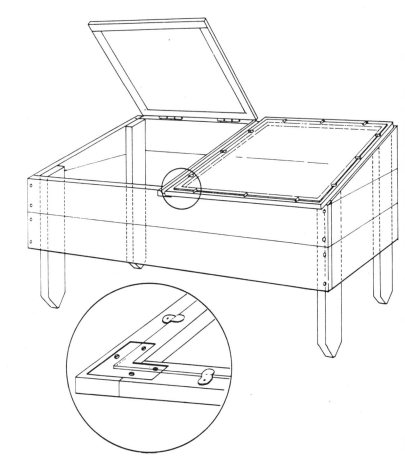

Propagation frame, with legs sunk into the ground for stability. Two lights cover the frame, made of either plastic or glass.

Seeds

Seed can be sown of any species that is not a hybrid and does not have a cultivar name in quotation marks. Seeds will usually come true to type for species i.e. those plants found in the wild. As soon as the seed is ripe, sow it immediately, and it will germinate readily. If sown any later it may take months to germinate. The exception to the rule is seed which ripens late in the season. Save this until about Christmas time, then sow for spring germination.

Use John Innes potting compost No 1 if sowing in mid-winter, or John Innes seed compost for spring and summer sowings. Use pots of not less than 3 in

Sowing fine alpine seeds into a clay pot filled with firm soil. The seed is mixed with dry sand to help spread the thinly sown seeds. Most seeds which are not so fine are sown direct from the hand.

(7.5 cm) diameter in plastic or clay, and fill with firmed soil to within $\frac{3}{4}$ in (2 cm) of the rim. Sow most seeds from the hand, not the packet, and thinly. Fluffy seeds can be teased over the soil, and large ones can be pushed into the soil individually. Very fine seeds are best mixed with dry horticultural sand, to give a thin and even distribution. With all seeds, use a single layer of small shingle or similar grains up to $\frac{5}{8}$ in (1.5 cm) in diameter to cover the seeds. No soil is necessary over the seeds. Water well, and plunge each pot almost up to the rim in the sand in the frame. Label each seed type before sowing, giving the name of the plant and date sown and place each label in its respective pot.

There is no need to cover the frame unless the weather is very wet. The cold does not matter; they are alpine seeds after all. Pot the seedlings up singly in small pots as soon as they are just large enough to handle. Grow on until they are large enough to plant.

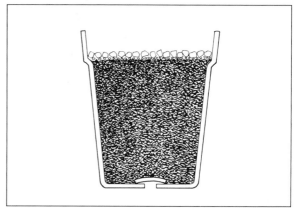

Cross-section of a pot sown with seeds. A crock covers the drainage hole, and a single layer of shingle covers the seeds. There is no need to cover them with soil first. The shingle will prevent the seeds from being washed out in heavy rain.

Cuttings

Use silver or horticultural sand and sieved peat in a 50/50 mixture, thoroughly soaking the peat first. Take cuttings of any hybrid plants, including those with names in quotes, or even species of wild origin where seed has not been produced. The cuttings can be taken at any time between June and August, but preferably by July to ensure hardening-off before the winter.

Nodal cuttings of young growth produced during the current year are the type taken. A node is the joint of a leaf or pair of leaves with the stem. Cut just below the leaf with a sharp knife to give a cutting up to 1 in (2.5 cm) long. Trim off the lowest leaves with a knife and insert the stem into the rooting compost of peat and sand, in a pot large enough for the number of cuttings to be taken. Use an old biro pen or knitting needle to do this. Water well and plunge the pot as for seeds in a frame. It is necessary to use a separate section of the frame for cuttings as the frame light will need to be left on all the time until they are rooted. Pot them up singly as for seedlings until well rooted for planting. Do remember to label each pot of cuttings.

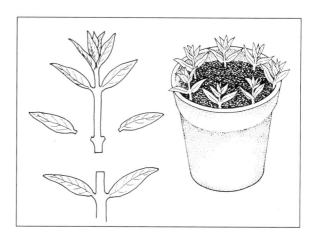

A nodal cutting, with the cut made just below a pair of leaves (node) and those leaves cut off. Nodal cuttings are then inserted into a mixture of 50% horticultural sand and 50% peat, and arranged round the outside of the pot.

As soon as the seedlings are germinated and the cuttings are rooted, move them into a frame with a cover on but with some air. The seed frame is fine for this purpose for about ten days, but they should then be moved into more light until large enough to plant.

Division

Herbaceous plants die down in the winter and should have their dead growth removed by March. When this is done, dig the plants up and take two hand forks, or border forks for bog plants which are bigger. Insert them back to back into the centre of the plant. Press down hard with both forks, then push the forks apart and this will split the plant. Throw away the centre parts, then repeat the process until a series of younger outside plants is produced. Use one or more of these to replant; spare ones will be available as swaps.

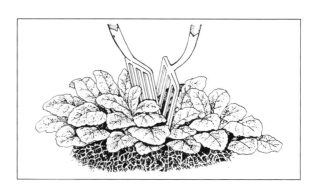

Index

This is John Warwick's second book on rock gardens. He is in charge of the rock garden and alpine house areas of the Royal Horticultural Society's Garden at Wisley in Surrey, having specialised in alpines since 1966. Before coming to Wisley he worked at a famous alpine nursery in Scotland. His time is now spent rebuilding the largest rock garden in Britain, and the alpine house area with all the frames and raised beds that go with it.